The Mission Through God's Eyes

By
Tracy Weakly

TEACH Services, Inc.
PUBLISHING
www.TEACHServices.com • (800) 367-1844

World rights reserved. This book or any portion thereof may not be copied or reproduced in any form or manner whatever, except as provided by law, without the written permission of the publisher, except by a reviewer who may quote brief passages in a review.

The author assumes full responsibility for the accuracy of all facts and quotations as cited in this book. The opinions expressed in this book are the author's personal views and interpretations, and do not necessarily reflect those of the publisher.

This book is provided with the understanding that the publisher is not engaged in giving spiritual, legal, medical, or other professional advice. If authoritative advice is needed, the reader should seek the counsel of a competent professional.

Copyright © 2013 TEACH Services, Inc.
ISBN-13: 978-1-4796-0217-9 (Paperback)
ISBN-13: 978-1-4796-0218-6 (ePub)
ISBN-13: 978-1-4796-0219-3 (Mobi)
Library of Congress Control Number: 2013948934

Published by

www.TEACHServices.com • (800) 367-1844

Dedication

This book is dedicated to my mother, Marcia Mollenkopf, for the many hours she spent listening, critiquing, and encouraging.

I wish to thank my children for their patience while I worked on this manuscript.

I share my appreciation for all those who read the manuscript and provided feedback.

Table of Contents

Introduction 7

Chapter 1   The Mission 9

Chapter 2   The Mission Is Born 11

Chapter 3   The Mission Matures 22

Chapter 4   The Mission Begins 30

Chapter 5   The Mission of God's Kingdom 41

Chapter 6   Mission of Hope 50

Chapter 7   Mission of Power 56

Chapter 8   Mission to the Unwanted 66

Chapter 9   The Final Mission Begins 74

Chapter 10   The Mission Unfolds 85

Chapter 11   The Mission Challenged 91

Chapter 12   The Mission Completed 103

Chapter 13   The Mission Triumphant 111

Chapter 14   The Mission Continues 122

Introduction

As I was studying the Bible, I asked God to show me more of His character. I wanted to see His incredible love in the painful times of my life as well as in the good times. My study led me to the four Gospels.

For each story recorded in the Gospels, I read a variety of sources and commentaries so as to gain a more complete picture of the culture that may have affected each situation. Then I read several versions of the Bible.

Contemplating what I had learned, I tried to imagine how a triune God experienced the events as portrayed in the Gospels. My purpose was to understand God's love. The Bible does not provide the conversations of the Trinity, or first-person accounts of their redemptive work for the human race. I have intentionally used masculine pronouns for all three members of the Godhead, since that is how they are recorded in the Bible. Accounts vary among the Gospels. While I have chosen to portray events in the best order possible, some stories have been moved to fit the chapter themes.

Also, I wanted to add a personal touch to each of the members of the Godhead as well as distinguish their different roles and personalities. As we know from reading the Bible, there are many names used to describe God. I have chosen the following:

- God the Father – I chose the name Yahweh, meaning, the Lord Jehovah, because it is most often used to represent the Supreme God over all.
- God the Son – I chose the name Yeshua because it is the Hebrew name for Jesus, the name He received when He became a man.
- God the Holy Spirit – I chose the name El-Shaddai, meaning, the All-Sufficient One, because it would portray best the Holy Spirit's role as a comforter.

As you read, I hope the message of God's love will shine through the stories and conversations in this book. The message is simple—each member of the Trinity loves us so much that each is intimately involved in our salvation. They work together as a unit, and yet separately in their uniqueness, to develop an eternal, saving relationship with every willing person.

It is my greatest desire that you will fall deeper in love with the Triune God who is deeply in love with you. May you be blessed as you journey with me through the Gospels, experiencing *The Mission Through God's Eyes*.

Chapter 1

The Mission

The celebration was incredible. The angelic choir had been practicing for ages for this performance. Gabriel had sung a special song he had written. Creatures from other worlds and universes had gathered in celebration and praise. Even the planets and stars seemed to sing a song of hope and adoration.

Yahweh, Yeshua, and El-Shaddai sang a new song with impressive harmony that stirred the hearts of all present. Each listener knew this might be the last time this harmony would ever be heard. The mission was so dangerous, the risk so great, the cost so high. Many wondered, *Were they, the inhabitants of planet earth, worth it?* Yet, if anyone questioned the mission, one only had to look at the Trinity, for the light, compassion, and love that emanated from them encircled all those present and reached out into the celestial realm beyond. Yes! The descendants of Adam and Eve had to know and experience that incredible, infinite love!

Yahweh, Yeshua, and El-Shaddai stood as the inhabitants of heaven and the other planets said goodbye, hugging them and offering blessings. Gabriel patiently waited until the end. As one of the head angels, he had worked most closely with Yeshua. Grabbing him in an all-encompassing embrace, Yeshua spoke softly, "You will be part of this mission."

"I know," Gabriel nodded. "But it will be so different. I will see you, but you …" His voice trailed off, unable to complete the horrific thought. "Oh, Yeshua, I love you."

Yeshua held him even closer. "I love you too, Gabriel." Then putting a strong hand on Gabriel's shoulder, Yeshua added, "It is time for your mission to begin. You have done well in meeting with Zachariah and Elizabeth. Now you must go. Mary is waiting for you, although she does not know it yet." Yeshua smiled such a contagious grin that Gabriel could not help but smile back. As Gabriel left for his assignment, Yeshua turned to Yahweh and El-Shaddai. "Shall we?"

Utilizing their omnipresence, the Three spent their last few moments revisiting memories since the beginning of time. They laughed as they shared the incredible joy of the creation of a galaxy called the Milky Way, the formation of its different planets and stars, and finally the delicate design of a special planet called earth. Eagerly they shared the times they had spent with Adam and Eve in the garden. They cried together as they talked of the fall, in which Adam and Eve had allowed darkness to invade where light had once reigned, not only in their hearts, but in their world as well. Their agonizing cries told of the pain at the separation of their human friends. They had known that humans might make this choice, so a plan had already been in place before creation had even begun. Death would be a reality for humans, but not an eternal one.

Yahweh, Yeshua, and El-Shaddai clasped hands together in a powerful grip as they mourned for those who had chosen the darkness. They desired that all would find peace in a relationship with them. As they walked among the stars, they recounted cherished memories of those who had accepted their love and friendship: Adam and Eve, Noah, Abraham, Joseph, Moses, David, Daniel—there were so many. After reviewing the past, they journeyed into the future and watched the final events of earth's history unfold. But for now, the mission must begin.

Hiding their light, they approached the dark blue and green sphere called earth. Entering the atmosphere, they moved toward the small village of Nazareth where a young woman named Mary was talking with Gabriel.

"He is so good with people," Yahweh said, smiling proudly. "I love watching him work."

"Yes," Yeshua agreed. Then turning toward Mary, he looked lovingly into her face. "I have been watching her since she was a baby. I enjoy the times she shares with us in her walks in the fields and hills. Now she has grown to become a beautiful woman." An amused grin spread across his face. "I have always called her my child, but from now on, I will call her Mother."

Yahweh nodded at the irony. "It is time," he said softly. Tears streamed down his face as he grasped Yeshua in a tight embrace. El-Shaddai encircled them, and their tears blended together, making tiny rainbows as they fell. After some time, Yahweh let go and gripped Yeshua's hands in his. Looking into each other's eyes, Yeshua spoke, "I love you, Father," he said. His smile matched that of Yahweh's. "I will be calling you that now. Abba Father."

Yahweh nodded. "And I will call you Son—you are my beloved son." Yahweh gripped Yeshua's shoulders. "I love you too, Son." They embraced one last time. Then they began the transformation.

Light encircled them as the creation of the body of the Creator began. The Three had worked on the pattern together. Carefully combining divinity with humanity, they wove together cellular structures into a perfectly formed egg. Yahweh gently held the tiny egg in his hand. El-Shaddai nodded. They looked around as amazed angels had gathered to watch, breathless and awed. "I love you, Son," Yahweh said softly as he handed the divine egg to El-Shaddai. Filling the egg with his presence, El-Shaddai placed it into Mary's womb. Yahweh lingered. Placing his hand on Mary, he whispered, *Take good care of him for me. I love him very much.* Then Yahweh joined El-Shaddai as the angels sang while accompanying them back to the throne room in heaven. Yahweh and El-Shaddai joined in the anthem, blending together in both sadness and joy, for the third part of their harmony was now missing.

Chapter 2

The Mission Is Born

Yahweh watched as Mary labored to give birth to his son. When Joseph had realized that Mary was in labor, he had sent for some local women in town to assist with the birth. Now two older women, one on each side, helped Mary stay in a squatting position with the aid of a birthing stool. Another woman, the midwife, coached Mary as each contraction brought the Son of God closer to his entrance into the world. El-Shaddai put his hand on Yahweh's shoulder. "He is almost here," he whispered. Yahweh nodded. Mary gave a cry as the baby crowned. Another push and his tiny head emerged. As the midwife gently held the baby's head, Mary gave her final push, and the Creator of the world now rested in the hands of the created. Tears filled Yahweh's eyes as he looked into Yeshua's innocent, sweet face.

The ambience was broken by the cries of the women. "Oh, Mary, you are so blessed. God has given you a son."

Mary nodded wearily. "I know," she said softly. "I know."

The midwife handed the baby to one of the older women. Carefully she washed him, rubbed him with salt, and wrapped him in strips of cloth to keep him warm and secure. Meanwhile, the other woman, along with the midwife, helped Mary finish the birthing process. They cleaned her and made her comfortable on a thin mat. Carefully they covered her with a warm blanket of animal skins.

Yahweh watched as Joseph was brought in and handed the swaddled baby. El-Shaddai nudged Yahweh. "Look at Joseph. He looks so proud."

"He should be," Yahweh said, grinning. "He is holding the Son of God."

"Yes," Gabriel spoke. "But he cannot even grasp what that really means."

"True," Yahweh replied. "However, his understanding will grow. Right now, all he needs is trust and a willingness to obey."

Gabriel looked around. The area was small, but it was swept as clean as possible. It seemed incomprehensible. "Even the richest palace on earth could not be an honorable enough place for Yeshua to be born, but here? It is so …"

"Humble?" Yahweh smiled knowingly.

Gabriel nodded. Yahweh rested his hand on Gabriel's shoulder. "Mary and Joseph are very grateful for the accommodations. Remember, they are considered peasants."

"And Yeshua will be a peasant too," Gabriel said with a sigh.

"Yes, if Yeshua is to reach even the poor, he must experience their life," Yahweh said softly. "Everyone, from the poor to the rich, must have the opportunity to be saved."

Turning away from Gabriel, Yahweh looked longingly at his son nestled in Mary's arms. Joseph rested beside her with one arm around her and the other gently playing with the baby's soft, brown hair.

Joseph turned to Mary and smiled. "Yeshua," he said softly. "You are Yeshua, the chosen Messiah." Mary nodded.

Yahweh smiled. The mission had begun.

* * * * *

Several angels who had been watching waited eagerly for their part of the mission. They had carefully composed the words and melody of the song that was to herald the Messiah's birth. It needed to be simple, yet elegant—a song that humans could understand and remember. Yahweh nodded to Gabriel.

Gabriel, accompanied by the angel choir, moved toward the fields outside of Bethlehem. El-Shaddai smiled. "I remember when David watched his father's sheep on these very hills."

"Yes," Gabriel replied. "I loved listening as he composed his songs of praise. Each song was unique and brought glory to Yahweh."

"Those songs guided him through many of the rough times in his life," Yahweh added.

They turned to watch a small group of shepherds exchanging places. Those who had finished their shift were going home, not knowing the significance of the hour. They, as well as most of the world, were ignorant that this seemingly normal night was anything but ordinary, for this new baby was about to change the world!

Yahweh laughed in anticipation. Little did this small group of shepherds know that they had been specifically chosen for tonight's watch. More than once, Yahweh had rearranged circumstances until the schedules of these chosen shepherds matched. These shepherds worked for the temple. It was their job to care for the temple sheep. Lambs bred from this flock were used for the temple sacrifices. What the unsuspecting shepherds did not know is that their task of guarding the flocks for Israel was about to change. They would soon be tasked with spreading good news to the *flock of Israel*.

The angel choir anxiously anticipated Gabriel's cue to begin singing, but Gabriel motioned to them to wait until everything was ready. Meanwhile, El-Shaddai moved in the hearts of the shepherds who had gathered near the resting sheep. These shepherds prayed for protection and safety for their night's work. Then they shared passages from the

Scriptures they had memorized. The favorite verses were those pointing to the promised Messiah, the Anointed One. It had been so long since there had been any prophet in Israel. The oppression from the Romans was taxing. It seemed that God was so far away. Yet in their darkness, hope shone forth, and their faith and trust in God was soon to be rewarded.

El-Shaddai smiled at Yahweh. Yahweh nodded to Gabriel. Slowly Gabriel moved toward the shepherds, now revealing his presence. Seeing the magnificent being of light, the shepherds were terrified. "Do not be afraid," Gabriel told them, "I have the most wonderful news to share with you and all people. Today, the Anointed One has been born in Bethlehem. You will find him wrapped in cloths and lying in a manger."

Gabriel nodded to cue the angelic choir. "All glory is given to God who is above all, for He has come to give peace on earth to His people."

The shepherds listened as the angels sang the simple chorus several times until the tune was firmly etched in their minds. As the angels' voices faded into the distance, the shepherds sat in awed silence as their eyes accustomed to the darkness of the night. Finally, the oldest shepherd spoke. "Come, let us go and see the new baby the angels told us about."

"What about the sheep?" the youngest asked.

The oldest shepherd put his hand on the young one's shoulder. "Do not worry about the sheep. I imagine one of those angels will watch them. We must listen and obey the words of the angel. God has chosen us."

Yahweh watched as the shepherds carefully made their way down the path that led to the town of Bethlehem. They kept singing the angel's chorus and following the light of the angels that led the way to the place where the young Messiah rested.

Upon reaching their destination, the oldest shepherd quietly knocked on the door. The door opened and a man asked, "May I help you?"

"Yes," the shepherd spoke. "We have come to see the baby."

Joseph nodded and waved a hand toward his wife and newborn son. "Come in. I am Joseph. This is my wife, Mary, and our newborn son. His name is Yeshua."

Yahweh observed as the shepherds who watched lambs reserved for sacrifice now knelt before the Lamb of God who would become the ultimate sacrifice. He grinned as he listened to the shepherds tell their story of the angels and everything that had happened that night. As they sang the song, baby Yeshua lay very still as if absorbing the significance of its words. El-Shaddai pressed close to Mary. *Remember this moment,* he spoke gently to her heart. *It will give you hope in the days ahead.*

It was late when the shepherds left. Quietly closing the door behind them, the oldest shepherd spoke. "God is wise. He knows that King Herod is very wicked, so He hid the Messiah among the poor rather than with the rich in a palace. He will be safest among us. It will also make him a good leader, for he will be familiar with the needs of the poor."

"How will he learn to be king?" the youngest shepherd asked.

"Have you forgotten about Moses or King David? God has his ways. He is very wise." Gabriel turned to Yahweh. "Yes, you are very wise." Yahweh smiled and nodded.

* * * * *

Slowly, reverently, Mary and Joseph entered the court of women on the outskirts of the magnificent temple. In one hand, Joseph held a small basket with two pigeons. With the other, he supported Mary, who was carrying their small son. It had been about forty days since that wonderful night he had been born. Now Mary entered the temple courtyard for her purification and the redemption of her firstborn son. The priest on duty was busy with another young family, so Mary and Joseph waited quietly, watching the activities of the priests and temple workers.

Yahweh smiled at El-Shaddai. "They have very little of the world's wealth, but they do everything they can to follow the laws we have given them."

"Yes," El-Shaddai nodded. "Yeshua was circumcised on the eighth day and given the name Gabriel instructed Mary to give him. He will be taught well."

The priest, once finished with the other family, motioned for Joseph and Mary to come forward with their offering. Taking the pigeons Joseph handed him, the priest broke the birds' necks and presented one as a burnt offering and the other as a sin offering. The priest recited the appropriate prayers for each. Then he nodded to Joseph who took the baby from Mary and placed him in the priest's arms.

"Look at his bright eyes," Yahweh said proudly to El-Shaddai. "He is already alert and learning so much. I can hardly wait until we can commune together. I have so much to share with him as he grows."

"I know," El-Shaddai nodded. "There will be much to share about the ways of the earth and what is happening around him."

Yahweh sighed. "I wish we could also share with him news of the universe, but that will have to wait until he rejoins us and takes his rightful place back in heaven. Then we will be able to catch up on the universal events he will have missed."

The priest began the ceremony, reminding Mary and Joseph of the importance of the dedication of the firstborn son to receive the birthright: the spiritual portion of priesthood and the double portion to care for his family.

"That priest does not have a clue as to the significance of the child he is holding," Gabriel said to Yahweh.

"I know," Yahweh said sadly. "Only those who have spiritual insight can truly see."

Gabriel gazed into the baby's eyes. "I suppose it is fitting that here among humans young Yeshua receives his mission. He will become their intercessor and priest. Now, about the double portion part, he already owns the cattle on a thousand hills, and the earth itself, and …" Gabriel grinned as he let the thought trail off.

The priest continued by reminding Mary and Joseph of the redemption of the firstborn son that began in Egypt when the angel of death passed over the doors of all who had the blood of the lamb on the doorposts. Since that time, all firstborn sons were to be redeemed for God's service.

"How ironic," Gabriel continued. "The baby who is being redeemed is the very one who will become the Lamb who will redeem all who choose him, even that priest who is holding him, and even Mary and Joseph who just did their part to redeem him."

The priest, seeing another couple waiting close by, concluded his ceremony with a blessing for male sons, which included the hope of the Messiah. He handed the baby back to Joseph. Then he wrote his name, Yeshua, on the scroll that documented the dedicated firstborn sons. He smiled politely and turned to face the next waiting family.

Another angel came close to Gabriel. "Everything is in place," he grinned. "I am so excited. I even got Simeon up a little early just to make sure he was ready."

El-Shaddai smiled. "Yes, I enjoyed reminding him of those Messianic prophecies this morning as he studied God's word. His heart is so ready." Simeon's guardian angel moved next to Simeon, guiding him toward Mary and Joseph just as the priest returned the baby to his mother.

Simeon was praying, as always, as he walked. His constant prayer was for the Messiah to come and redeem his people. *Simeon*, El-Shaddai spoke softly to his conscience, *the One for whom you have prayed for is here.* Simeon looked up. *He is right there.*

"Wait!" Simeon spoke loudly. Walking very quickly, he was soon by Mary's side. "May I?" Filled with El-Shaddai's presence, he took the young Messiah in his arms and gazed into the baby's face. Feeling the divine presence, the baby looked into Simeon's face. As Simeon watched, the prophecies he had studied became clear before his eyes.

Lifting the baby toward heaven, he prophesied, "Thank you, Lord, for keeping your promise to me. I can die now, knowing that the Redeemer of all has come. He will be a light in our darkness, a light even to the Gentiles."

Turning to Mary and Joseph, he continued. "God has blessed you and will continue to guide you in this great task he has given you." Simeon paused. His eyes softened as he focused on Mary. "This child will be accepted by many, but he will also be rejected by many more. When this happens, you will feel some of his pain too. Remember, this shows the response of the people to God's gift."

Nearby, another angel was leading an older woman toward the small group. Anna, now 84, had devoted her life to intercessory prayer. She had been praying in the court of women when El-Shaddai had spoken to her. *Anna, it is time to see the fulfillment of your prayers.* Joyfully, she had left her place of prayer and was now near the place where young babies were blessed.

Listening to Simeon, she looked to heaven. "Lord, who am I to be so blessed. Thank you." As Simeon finished his blessing, his eyes met Anna's. She held out her hands. Gently Simeon placed the young Messiah into her arms. Cradling the baby in her arms, she looked into his face. "Blessed are you my child. You are the Chosen One. May you accomplish all that God has required of you."

Gently she caressed his face. She kissed him lightly on the forehead. Smiling, she then placed the baby back into Mary's arms. "You are greatly blessed." Then lifting her arms to heaven she began to sing, "Praise the Lord. Great is his mercy and love. He has answered the prayers of Israel. The Anointed One has come!"

As Anna left Joseph and Mary to ponder what had just happened, she gladly shared the good news of the arrival of the promised Messiah with everyone she met. "The promised Messiah is here!" she exclaimed. "I got to hold him. Let me tell you about it …"

Gabriel chuckled. "Leave it to Anna."

Anna's angel laughed. "I love being her guardian. She is so full of love for God."

Gabriel grinned and nodded. "Well you should better get going. Anna is already hurrying down the steps."

As Anna's guardian moved to her side, Gabriel turned to watch Mary and Joseph. As Mary looked into her baby's eyes, Yahweh whispered in his son's ear. *You are my beloved son. You are truly blessed. You are part of a great mission that we will accomplish together. I love you, Son. I love you.*

* * * * *

It was an odd sight around Jerusalem that day. Camels and Arabian horses were loaded with supplies, revealing the long journey from which they had come. Several distinguished men rode atop the large animals, accompanied by servants and guards who ensured they had a comfortable and safe journey. Their clothes were a blend of exquisite colors, including the rare dyes of purple and blue. These men were definitely leading figures of royalty in the country from which they had come. Judging from their appearances, they came from the east, maybe from Babylon, Persia, or Arabia. The caravan paused at the gate of the city and requested admission. The gatekeeper nodded his approval of the prominent gentlemen and let them enter. Eagerly they left the caravan and entered the city.

"Excuse me," one of the gentlemen said, approaching the elder who sat near the gate. "We are looking for the one who is born King of the Jews. Do you know where we might find him?"

The elder looked puzzled, so a second man continued. "We have been following the great star that indicates an important leader. We have come to pay our respects in worship."

Realizing that the elder did not seem to know about the young king, the astute visitors walked through the streets of Jerusalem seeking answers to their quest.

Gabriel turned to Yahweh. "They have come so far. I hope they do not become discouraged."

"Their faith has brought them here," Yahweh answered. "It may be shaken, but hope will keep them going until they accomplish their quest."

"I have really enjoyed traveling with them," El-Shaddai ventured. "They have followed all the light they have been given. I am so eager to share even more with them as they continue on their journey."

The wise men had been searching for some time when they turned a corner and headed toward the marketplace. As they approached the busy market, a young messenger from the palace approached them. Bowing respectfully, he delivered this message. "King Herod has heard of your quest. He has consulted with the Jewish leaders and now wishes to have a private interview with you."

Delighted, the men of royalty followed the young messenger through the streets until they arrived at a magnificent palace. They were ushered inside and escorted to a large room where Kind Herod was waiting.

"Greetings of peace from our country to yours," one of the men spoke as they bowed politely. "We are magi from the east. We are skilled in astrology, magical arts, and wisdom. We follow the great Persian teacher Zoroaster who taught that a great ruler would come, who will triumph over chaos, which will be completed in a final restoration of the world."

The spokesman continued, "Several months ago we saw an astrological phenomenon in the springtime night sky."

Herod leaned forward. "How did this discovery bring you here?"

"We wanted to know the meaning of the phenomenon, so we went back to the writings of the great wise teachers from the time of the Persian Empire. There we read the writings of a wise counselor by the Hebrew name of Daniel. He told of an Anointed One who would sit on a throne and judge the earth. He stated clearly in the interpretation of a dream that Nebuchadnezzar had that the Anointed One's kingdom will last forever. Then we found an ancient scroll of a magician named Balaam. He wrote that a star, a great king would come from the land of the Hebrews. That night we saw the unknown, unexplainable star of celestial light. We have been following it for many months, and it has led us here."

Pausing, the wise leader presented his request. "Now, honorable King Herod, we have come to pay our respects to this great king who has been born. Where may we find him so that our quest may be completed and we may journey back to our country?"

Gabriel smiled briefly at the conclusion of their speech, but he shuddered, for he could feel an evil presence around Herod's throne. "Herod is so paranoid that someone will take his throne. He has already executed one of his wives, several relatives, and even his sons. I hate to think what he will plot next."

"He can only do what Yahweh will allow," El-Shaddai reminded him.

Herod smiled politely, but in his mind he was devising his next scheme. "I questioned the priests of the Jewish people. They told me of a prophecy that indicates that the great king's birthplace is in Bethlehem. Try looking there, and when you find the young king, please let me know where he is so I too can worship him." He stroked his beard, pleased with himself that his plan seemed to outsmart even the wisest men from the east.

"Thank you," the wise one said while bowing respectfully before King Herod. The others followed. The young messenger led them out of the palace and back through the city streets to the gate where the caravan waited anxiously. As the night began to close around them, one of the magi looked up into the night sky at the stars that were beginning to penetrate the darkness. "Look!" he cried eagerly. "It is the star, and it appears to be in the direction of Bethlehem."

* * * * *

"Look at him," Yahweh said proudly to El-Shaddai. "Can you believe it? He is already walking!" They watched as young Yeshua grabbed a three-legged stool, pulling himself up to a standing position. His bright eyes gazed up at Mary who was standing close by. She held out her hands. "Come here, Yeshua. Come to Mommy," she beckoned in excitement. The young Yeshua cooed in delight, took three unsteady steps, and sat down abruptly by Mary's feet. Mary scooped him up in her arms and swung him around, the two laughing together.

"Mary," Joseph suddenly appeared in the doorway of the house where they were staying, "we have visitors. They are here to see the young king of Israel." His eyes twinkled as he spoke.

Mary sat down on the stool and placed baby Yeshua in her lap. Several distinguished gentlemen bowed as they entered the house. Mary had never seen anyone so lavishly dressed. She knew these men were royalty, although she could not be sure what country they were from.

The men knelt upon the floor of their humble home. They bowed low as one would before someone of much greater status. Joseph sat next to Mary as the two watched in utter amazement. They were poor and did not expect to receive honor from those of such high status.

Remember, Mary, Yahweh spoke to her heart, *the one you hold on your lap is greater even than the kingly magi before you. He is the King of kings.*

The magi sat up but remained in a kneeling position. One of them motioned to a servant who was waiting by the door. "The gifts," he said. The servant nodded and left. Soon he came back carrying a bag of fine leather. One of the magi graciously took the bag and placed it near Mary's feet. "I have brought gold for the king." He looked at Joseph and Mary, waiting for the acceptance of his gift.

"Thank you," Joseph said modestly. "Your gift is honorable."

Another gentleman placed his gift, a small, but elegantly carved box, in front of the young couple. He lifted the lid. Inside chunks of amber resin rested in blue cloth. "Frankincense," the wise one stated, "a fragrant gift for the young king."

"Your gift is most gracious," Joseph replied.

The third man placed a flask of fine clay painted in a mosaic pattern before Joseph and Mary. "Myrrh," he said, "for the young king's anointing."

"Your gift is most worthy," Joseph acknowledged.

The magi smiled and repositioned themselves cross-legged upon the floor.

Gabriel looked into Yahweh's face. "The gifts are fitting," he began. "Gold is the gift for kings, especially the King of kings. Frankincense is incense used on the altar, which speaks to Yeshua's priestly ministry. Myrrh is not only for anointing at the beginning of the mission, but it signals the preparation of his body for burial after the crowning act of the mission."

El-Shaddai nodded. "Joseph and Mary don't yet understand the full significance of each gift, but they do have the divine assurance that Yeshua is the Messiah and that Yahweh will provide for their needs as they take care of such a special gift from heaven."

Mary placed young Yeshua on the floor. Curious, he began to play with the leather strap securing the gold. Mary gently moved him away from the gold and directed him toward the magi. One of the magi held out his hand to the young king. Young Yeshua grasped his hand, pulled himself up, and toddled a few steps. Then he sat down, crawled into the gentleman's lap and began to play with the trimming at the edge of the richly decorated robe. Mary started to intervene, but the magi just shook his head.

"We must tell our story," the magi began. Joseph nodded, and the magi began. "We are magi from the east …"

*****

It was late when the men finished their visit, bowed politely, and left. They joined their caravan and left the town, traveling just a short distance to the outskirts of Bethlehem where they found a place to camp. They would begin their journey home in the morning.

Yahweh watched the men as they slept. He loved each one. They did not completely know him or understand his teachings, yet they listened to his voice and unquestionably followed his directions. They had traveled a long distance to worship Yeshua, but their mission was not complete. Yahweh nodded to El-Shaddai.

El-Shaddai moved close to the one who had been the spokesman to King Herod and spoke to him through a dream. *Be careful, my friend*, he warned. *Do not tell King Herod you have found the young boy. Herod is an evil man. He has killed all those he thought might take his crown. He will try to kill the child too.*

The magi awoke, a cold sweat covering his body. "It makes sense now. The young king must be hidden among the poor. That is why no one seems to know about him. He must be kept safe or else King Herod will kill him." He lay back down on his mat. "We will go home a different way," he murmured as he fell back to sleep.

* * * * *

Gabriel flew to where Joseph and Mary lay sleeping on a mat with the young Yeshua beside them. Yahweh nodded, acknowledging the urgency of the message. "The time has come," he told Gabriel. Gabriel appeared to Joseph in a dream. *Wake up*, he said. *Quickly take Mary and the young child and go to Egypt. King Herod has soldiers already on the way to kill him. You must stay in Egypt until I tell you to return.*

Joseph awoke, startled. "Mary!" He shook her firmly. "An angel came to me in a dream. We must leave immediately and go to Egypt. King Herod is sending soldiers to kill Yeshua."

Together they rolled up the mat they were sleeping on and gathered a few basic belongings. Then Joseph carried the precious gifts the magi had brought. "God always provides," he smiled. Placing the young child in Mary's arms, they began the eighty-mile journey to the Egyptian border. From there, they would travel to Alexandria where many Jews had settled during the Diaspora.

Yahweh watched as the family began their journey under the cover of darkness. The smoothness of the road and the brightness of the stars would guide their way. Angels walked beside them, ensuring their journey would be a safe one. However, Yahweh knew it would not be safe for everyone.

* * * * *

Herod paced the floor of his throne room. He had given the magicians plenty of time to find the king and return, but they had not come. "They have disobeyed me!" he shouted to no one in particular. He replayed in his mind the events of that day when the magi had visited Jerusalem. "They had such a large caravan," he mused. "Their country must be spying on me. They must be planning an attack!" Seeing a three-legged stool nearby, he kicked it across the floor. It splintered to a halt against a low table. "Somebody must pay!" he screamed.

Then he remembered the Jewish leaders. *They seemed hesitant to tell me any details about the young king. Are they really that ignorant? Of course not! They are planning a revolt.*

I will show them that no one defies King Herod. No one attempts to take my throne! "Call the captain of the guard!" he ordered to a nearby servant. "Tell him to send a group of soldiers to Bethlehem. Have them find every male child under two years old and kill him. No one shall take my throne!"

Gabriel stood beside Yahweh as King Herod belted out the horrific orders. Yahweh turned to Gabriel. "We must allow the massacre. It has been foretold in the books of the prophets. However, send extra guardians to Bethlehem. We must be near the families to comfort and strengthen them through this catastrophic event." Gabriel nodded. He was too numb to speak. Oh how he wished this evil would end. It was so painful to witness its effects. As he turned to go, his eyes met the eyes of Yahweh. Tears were streaming down his face too.

Chapter 3

The Mission Matures

"He has grown so much these last few years," Yahweh spoke to El-Shaddai. "I love his bright eyes and warm smile."

"Yes," El-Shaddai nodded. "He is so eager to learn, quick to help, and willing to share."

"Mommy, thank you for sharing the story of the young boy Samuel with me. I like hearing it over and over again," Yeshua said as he pressed close to Mary, her arms around him. He always enjoyed the stories Mary taught him from Scripture.

Mary smiled. "What is your favorite part?" she asked, already knowing his answer. It was always the same, but she still enjoyed hearing it.

"I like it when God talked to Samuel." Yeshua's eyes glistened as he spoke. "He was only a boy, but God talked to him. Do you think God will talk to me too?"

"I am sure he will," Mary said as she embraced her young son.

"How will I know God is talking to me?" Yeshua's eyes looked deeply into hers.

"You will know," Mary replied, her eyes looking beyond to a memory of not so long ago.

The young Yeshua gently pulled on her sleeve. "Tell me when God talked to you, when the angel came and told you about …"

Mary laughed. "Okay, but only while we are making bread, or we will have nothing for supper." Mary grabbed the young boy's hand, and they skipped toward the courtyard where the coals of the fire were ready for baking.

* * * * *

It was early morning when the young Yeshua walked along the edge of the field near his home. A small chirping caught his attention. Ever so carefully, he walked toward the sound. It was a young sparrow stranded on the ground, loudly chirping for its parents to rescue it from its plight.

"Poor little bird," Yeshua whispered softly to the sparrow. People walked past, hurrying to accomplish the tasks of a new day. "No one seems to care."

I do, Yahweh whispered softly in Yeshua's ear. *I see the sparrow fall. I care about every living creature.*

Yeshua looked around, but saw no one. *Look at the lilies near your feet*, Yahweh continued.

Yeshua picked up a flower and looked carefully at each petal. "It's very pretty," he said softly.

Thank you, Yahweh smiled. *I made it.*

Yeshua had begun recognizing Yahweh's voice impressing on his heart. "It looks like most people are too busy to see the flowers or this bird," Yeshua said. "But you see them, right? And you take care of them because they belong to you. No one is here to help me, but I need to put this baby bird back in its nest." Yeshua continued talking to Yahweh as he picked up the baby sparrow and tried to put it in the tree. "I am going to need your help."

Yahweh grinned and winked at El-Shaddai. Yeshua climbed the tree onto a low-hanging branch with his chirping friend. He scooted across the branch until he was near enough to the nest to put the bird inside. Satisfied the bird was safe, Yeshua inched toward the trunk and descended until he could safely jump to the ground. Once his two feet were on the ground, he brushed himself off. Looking up, he smiled. "Thank you," he said as he grabbed three lilies and ran toward home.

As he burst into the courtyard, he exclaimed, "Mommy, look!" Mary put down the basket she was carrying. "Look at the flowers. God made them. They are very pretty. We must not be too busy to see them."

Mary carefully examined the flowers in her son's hands. "Yes, they are very pretty."

Looking into his mother's eyes, Yeshua continued, a serious note to his voice. "God takes care of them. He takes care of us too." Then he ran off to get a small container to put them in, leaving Mary still holding the flowers.

Mary sighed, "Sometimes I do not understand that boy."

Yahweh grinned at El-Shaddai, and they both laughed.

* * * * *

"Daddy!" Yeshua ran through the door of the carpentry shop. Joseph put down his tools and grabbed his young son and swung him around. "How was school?"

Yeshua sat on a stool near Joseph's table. "I love school. The teacher says I am learning quickly. I can read parts of the Torah now. I love memorizing. Today I recited three chapters from Leviticus without any help."

Joseph grinned at his son, but before he could say anything Yeshua continued. "I sang part of Psalm 119 today. Now I understand why King David said we must hide God's word in our hearts—so that God's word is always with us. I want to memorize the entire Torah and as many scriptures as I can."

Joseph put his hand on Yeshua's shoulder. "I am sure you will. Why don't you recite one of those chapters while you help me with the table I am finishing."

Yahweh listened intently as Yeshua recited the words he himself had spoken to Moses many centuries before. *Yes, Son, keep those words in your heart. They will guide you for the journey ahead.*

* * * * *

The young Yeshua rested on a rock at the edge of the field. When he met Yahweh and El-Shaddai here, he often discussed with them the inconsistencies of the culture around him.

You look discouraged, Yahweh said, moving closer to where Yeshua was sitting, *it looks like it was a rough day.*

Yeshua nodded. *On the way to school, I divided my lunch with Elias, the blind beggar who sits by the gates near the temple. I felt so sorry for him. Then I helped a woman carry her basket to her house. It looked so heavy. During the noon meal I shared a little fish with a stray dog that was scrounging for food.*

Sounds like an honest day's work, Yahweh spoke in approval. *However, I imagine others did not think so.*

Yeshua shook his head. *Mother was concerned that I had given away part of my lunch. She said the beggar was blind because he must have done something wrong and that you were punishing him.* He paused. *That doesn't sound like something you would do.*

And the woman? Yahweh queried.

The teacher scolded me for helping the woman who was a lower status than I, which caused me to be late for school. Yeshua shook his head in disgust. *And the dog? Well, I was told it was foolish to waste my fish on a dog.*

Yeshua tossed a pebble onto the sandy ground beside him. *I believe the Torah says that mankind is supposed to take care of the animals.*

Yahweh laughed. *You are right. It started in the very beginning when Adam named the animals.*

Yeshua's face grew serious. *What about people? I cannot believe you created a caste system. And what about diseases or calamities? Do sins have a caste system too? What makes Elias' sin so bad that he is blind, but when a band of robbers stole from our neighbor's farm, they were not struck blind. Besides, if sin is so bad, people who are sinful could never pay a price big enough to redeem themselves. Could you explain this to me?*

Yahweh drew near. *Look at the world of nature. Is everything created the same?*

No, Yeshua held out his hand as a small bug crawled onto it.

Is one more important than another? Yahweh queried.

No, each is created differently, but each works together as part of a whole. He put the bug on a leaf of a shrub near him. *This plant shares its leaves with the bug, and the bug shares its life for the bird ...* Yeshua paused, letting the thought sink in. *Similarly, people have different jobs. No one is better than the other. We all work together for the glory of God.*

Yahweh grinned. *That is correct.*

What about diseases and calamities? Yeshua ventured.

When did these things begin on earth? Yahweh asked.

The Torah says that things began to die after Adam and Eve ate the fruit in the garden. Yeshua paused. *So Elias is blind, not because of his sin, but because of the first sin? In other words, bad things happen because this world is full of sin?*

You are correct. Yahweh pressed further. *If people cannot pay for their sins by being blind or having leprosy, how can they?*

Yeshua thought for a moment. *By the sacrifice of the lamb.*

Yahweh nodded. *Continue to study and all will come clear to you.*

Yeshua stood up. *I will continue to study the Scriptures. In the meantime, I guess I need to keep helping others even if I sometimes get in trouble.*

Show them my true character. Share with them my love, Yahweh answered. *That is the only way they will understand.*

Yeshua stepped onto the path toward home. *Thank you, Father.*

I love you, Son, Yahweh replied.

* * * * *

"I look forward to this time of year," Gabriel exclaimed as he grinned at Yahweh. "I love watching the people journey to the temple in Jerusalem for the Passover. I enjoy celebrating with them in singing and prayer, and joining them as they participate in ceremonies that are so rich with meaning. I wonder how many of them realize that the joy they are experiencing fellowshipping together is but a taste of the wonderful celebrations of worship we have in heaven."

Yahweh nodded. "I can hardly wait until the time when they will join in worship with all the heavenly beings."

"That will be amazing," El-Shaddai sighed. "And with each passing day we grow closer to that reality."

Gabriel nodded. He loved the way Yahweh and El-Shaddai worked in harmony, yet he missed not having Yeshua around. Meanwhile, the young Yeshua was excitedly traveling with his family to attend his first Passover. Gabriel, Yahweh, and El-Shaddai listened in as Joseph conversed with his brother.

"I am very excited about this Passover celebration," Joseph said to his brother, whose family had joined them in the journey toward Jerusalem. "Yeshua is twelve. He has already begun preparing for his bar mitzvah ceremony."

"I am sure he will do fine." Joseph's brother kept his step in time with Joseph's. "He is very bright and good with memorization."

"I know," Joseph admitted. "He did well in school while learning to read, memorize, and understand the Torah and the other Scriptures, but when he started learning the oral traditions, he lost interest. He has been finishing his studies at home. Rabbi Abraham has been very understanding though. He says some boys need to question everything in order to understand all things."

"He seems like a wise rabbi," Joseph's brother added.

"He is," Joseph admitted. "He allows Yeshua to come and read from the Scriptures during times when school is not in session. And he has offered to help Yeshua with his readings and study preparation. I am hoping, though, that celebrating the Passover in Jerusalem, seeing the temple services, and listening to the great rabbis and priests will give Yeshua a clearer understanding of the Jewish traditions."

"I hope so too," Gabriel mused, "but not in the way Joseph intends." Turning to Yahweh he added. "The mission with all its demands is such a heavy weight for a young lad to carry."

Yahweh nodded. "Yes, but everything will be revealed in portions he can understand and will be able to handle. I will not give him more than he can bear at one time."

"We are almost there!" A shout could be heard from someone toward the front of the group. Someone began to sing one of the psalms of assents. Others joined in. "I was overjoyed when they invited me, 'let us go to God's house.' Now we are here. We are standing inside the gates of Jerusalem." The singing continued. "Pray for peace for Jerusalem and her people."

Yahweh smiled proudly. "I love hearing young Yeshua sing. His voice is so clear, not yet mature, but getting there."

El-Shaddai agreed. "And the love that flows from his heart is so genuine it blends beautifully with the melody."

"Yes, especially today." Gabriel watched as Yeshua stood in awe as they neared the temple. For a human-crafted building, it was magnificent in both size and beauty. Its neatly carved white stones formed the walls. Marble pillars supported the vast ceilings. Pure gold accentuated the decorated carvings. Gold was also the medium by which the temple furniture was made. The temple itself was enormous with many courts and places for people to perform ceremonies or worship. Yet, young Yeshua was not interested in its outward beauty. Instead, he was searching for something greater—he was searching for its meaning.

* * * * *

The Mission Matures

Yahweh stood close to his son throughout the ceremonies of the next few days. El-Shaddai, too, stayed close, listening to Yeshua's questioning thoughts and helping him to understand. There was so much for him to learn. During the Seder, he contemplated the meaning of each symbol. There was the service itself, which signaled the Israelites deliverance from Egypt. There were cups of wine, bitter herbs, charoset, and three matzos with one broken, hidden, then found. Everyone seemed to be talking about freedom from Rome and the bitterness of its rule. But to Yeshua it seemed that a spiritual redemption from spiritual slavery was more important than a physical redemption from Rome.

Then there was the shofar that had sounded in the early afternoon. As the priest placed the sins of Israel on the lamb and sacrificed it, the people were required to contemplate their sins and ask for forgiveness. But as Yeshua saw the lamb, it began to make sense. The meaning of the Passover was not the suffering of the people, but the suffering of the lamb. However, Yeshua realized that the sacrificial lamb was but a symbol of the Lamb of God. It was the Lamb who would drink the cup of the wine of God's wrath. It was the Lamb who would taste the bitterness of suffering. Yes, it was the Lamb who would be broken as a sacrifice, hidden, and then found. The Lamb brought true redemption. As the realization flooded his body, Yeshua sought to be alone. Slowly, reverently he made his way to a secluded spot where few people were gathered. Yahweh pressed close to his son, wrapping his presence around him while El-Shaddai filled Yeshua with his presence within.

As Yeshua slowly walked along the temple wall, he began reciting passages from Isaiah. "He was led like a lamb to be sacrificed. The Lord placed on Him all of our sins." Looking up, he cried softly, "Oh Father, the Anointed One, he is the lamb."

Yes, my son, Yahweh gently spoke to his heart. *The Messiah must first become the lamb for all, then the priest for all, then the king of all.*

* * * * *

Yahweh watched as several young men sat in a semicircle around the great teachers of the temple who were listening and debating issues. Among them was Yeshua.

"Notice that young man in the middle of the group?" One of the rabbis leaned over to another rabbi nearest him and whispered in his ear. "Who is he? I have not seen him in our schools before."

"Would you believe he is from Nazareth? I talked to a relative of his this morning. I guess his family came for Passover, and he is staying with relatives so he can learn more."

"He is amazingly bright and inquisitive," the first rabbi continued, "especially since he came from Galilee. Their schools are not of the same caliber as ours."

"True, maybe if he came to our schools he would become a great teacher in Israel," the second rabbi agreed.

"Oh, he will be a great teacher in Israel," Gabriel said to El-Shaddai. "And He will not need their help."

"Now, Gabriel," El-Shaddai nudged Gabriel playfully.

"The ignorance of humans is sometimes annoying," Gabriel commented. "Yeshua, the student, has been teaching the teachers for two days now, and they do not even see it."

"I know," Yahweh said. "It is sad. They could know so much if only they could see."

Just then, two people entered the temple classroom. Seeing Yeshua, Mary sighed with relief. Quietly, so as not to interrupt, Joseph and Mary sat behind the young scholars and listened. Yeshua was talking with the great teacher about passages written by the prophet Isaiah. "The prophet says that 'he is led like a lamb to be sacrificed.' Who is the prophet talking about? What does the prophet mean when he says 'the Lord placed on him all of our sins'?"

"What do you think?" one of the great teachers asked in return. It was common for great philosophers to answer questions with another question, helping the student to think clearly and seek understanding of truth.

El-Shaddai's presence filled Yeshua as divinity shone through humanity. "The one whom God has chosen," Yeshua answered.

"I have not seen him debate philosophy before," Joseph whispered to Mary. "He is truly amazing."

In spite of the anxiety of the last few days and the frustration that was welling up inside her as to how Yeshua could have disappeared without telling them, Mary nodded in agreement. "Yes, he has the wisdom of God."

Seeing the couple, the teachers paused the session. Joseph motioned to Yeshua that it was time to leave. Yeshua rose, politely thanked the teachers, and followed his parents out of the room.

When they reached the passageway leading toward another section of the temple, Mary stopped and grabbed her son. Looking into his eyes, she let out all of the pent up emotions she had been holding inside. "How could you make us worry like this? We did not know where you were!"

As Yeshua placed his hand on her shoulder, Mary realized something in him had changed. The mature boy who had arrived in Jerusalem had somehow become a young man by the end of the trip. He now carried a new weight on his shoulders, an understanding in his heart, and a look of resolve on his face. "Mother," he spoke gently, "why were you looking for me? Do you not understand? I need to be with God, my true Father, in his house, preparing for the mission he has called me to do."

Mary looked at Joseph. He nodded. They accepted what they could not fully understand. Yeshua wrapped one arm around each of his earthly parents. "I am ready now. Let us go home."

"It is so hard to be human," Yahweh said. "From now on Mary and Joseph will have to trust even more than ever."

"Yes," El-Shaddai said, placing his hand on Yahweh's shoulder. "And Yeshua will have to blend both worlds into one."

Chapter 4

The Mission Begins

Yahweh watched as Yeshua carefully cleaned the last few carpentry tools, organizing them neatly beside the workbench. Eighteen years had passed since that life-changing visit to Jerusalem. During those quiet years Yeshua had spent many hours in the fields and hills talking with Yahweh and El-Shaddai. They had discussed the mission, its meaning, and every detail involved. Even humanity could not hide the divine presence in Yeshua. The Three had become one in purpose, each carrying out his own unique task yet working simultaneously with the others, blending in perfect harmony.

Waiting provides time for people and events to be arranged in their designated places. It strengthens faith, ignites hope, and prepares the soul. Now the waiting was over. The time had come. Everything was in place. Yeshua had completed the work for his earthly father. Now it was time for him to begin the work of his heavenly Father.

Yeshua saw Mary in the courtyard. He watched as she adeptly mixed the bread dough. She formed a small ball with her hand, flattened it, and returned it to the bowl, repeating the process until the entire batch was shaped. Then she baked each piece over the low burning fire, turning each piece to make sure each side was evenly cooked. She placed each cooked piece onto a cloth that rested neatly in a basket.

Yeshua thought of the many years they had spent together. Even though she didn't completely understand his ways, his choices, or his mission, she had faith. She took her task seriously. Now she was getting older. Joseph had died, and Yeshua had done his part to care for her and the family business. Now Yeshua's brothers and sisters would need to do their share.

Yeshua put his hand on Mary's shoulder. "Mother," he said softly, "I have completed my work here. I feel the Spirit of God calling me."

Mary looked into his eyes, "Where will you go?"

"My cousin John is preaching and baptizing people in the Jordan River. I want to hear him," he stated.

Mary nodded. "I remember when Elizabeth was carrying him. It was a miraculous birth foretold by an angel. It was such a blessing to be with her when I was carrying you. You and John have much in common. It will be good for you to spend some time with

John."

"Thank you," Yeshua kissed his mother on the cheek. "Goodbye."

Mary handed him a round piece of the flatbread. "Here, take this with you."

Yeshua grinned and took the bread. "I love you, Mother."

* * * * *

John stood on the bank of the Jordan River. His tunic was woven from camel hair. The thick, dark cloth was waterproof. It was tied with a leather belt. "Please come," he preached. "Make a complete turn around in your lives. Turn away from sin and turn toward God. Come and be baptized. The Messiah is coming soon. We must be ready."

Yeshua walked slowly toward a group of people standing around John, listening to him preach. El-Shaddai moved close to John. *The one you are preparing the way for is here.* As John looked up, his eyes met Yeshua's. Divinity shone through humanity as Yeshua stepped forward. "Please, John," he smiled, "I would like for you to baptize me."

John did not know how to respond. "Why do you want to be baptized? You do not need forgiveness. You are the Sinless One. You do not need to prepare for the Messiah. You are the Anointed One. You are the Great Teacher. I am only a disciple. You should be baptizing me."

Yeshua spoke with conviction. "God's work of redemption through the centuries is coming together right now. God's cleansing will set me apart for his mission. His anointing will equip me to accomplish this mission. Let us work together to fulfill his righteous purpose."

John nodded. Reaching his hand out to Yeshua, the two walked into the middle of the river. Looking toward heaven, John prayed, *I humbly accept what you have asked me to do.* Then he submersed the Son of God under the water and brought him back upright.

As Yeshua stood up out of the water, he prayed, "Father, forgive these people. Make them open to your mission." In response, El-Shaddai's presence enveloped Yeshua, anointing him for the mission. Slowly El-Shaddai fashioned a piece of his glory into a visible shape of a dove that hovered above Yeshua's head.

Proudly and joyfully, Yahweh spoke. "This is my son, the Anointed One. I love him deeply. I am pleased and have accepted him."

An awed silence fell upon the small group as they witnessed the presence of a triune God. They knew that just as a father gave the family work to his son in the form of a covenant, so Yahweh had given Yeshua his work. Yeshua would represent Yahweh on earth by carrying out the work he had been given.

Yeshua nodded to John, and the two began to walk back to shore. As their feet touched the sandy bank, John said, "This is truly the Lamb of God. He will take away the sins of the world." As John spoke, Yeshua slipped away from the crowd and was gone.

* * * * *

It had been forty days since the baptism. Yeshua had found a secluded place in the hills near the Jordan River to talk with Yahweh and El-Shaddai. They had so much to share. They talked about people and events, prophecies, and meanings. But most of all, they talked about the mission.

Father, the mission before me is great. Yeshua rested against a tree as he spoke with his heavenly Father. *Our love is connected. If I am to represent you on earth, we must work together as one. Please fill me with your power and glory so I can complete the work. Thank you for showing yourself to me. Help me to show the world your true character. They need to see your love. Love the world through me. Then I can give back to you the glory you have given me.*

Yes, my son, Yahweh said. *I will always be with you even when you can not feel my presence. Faith can always see what seems hidden.*

El-Shaddai added. *My presence will always be in you, making my power immediately available.*

Thank you. Yeshua stood up and leaned against the tree. The light of their presence seemed to fade, but he knew they were still there. He was exhausted. He had so much to share and learn and understand. The communion among the Three had been so intense and engaging that simple tasks such as satisfying hunger had been ignored. Now, Yeshua's humanity was taking over.

Gabriel watched, staying close. He loved Yeshua and would make sure every human need was taken care of. Other angels waited nearby for orders.

Suddenly Gabriel felt an evil chill around him. Turning, he saw Lucifer walking close to Yeshua. Instead of hiding his presence, Lucifer made himself visible to Yeshua. He seemed to be a dazzling angel of light, but his words would soon betray him.

"If you are really the Son of God," Lucifer began, "use your power to turn these stones into bread."

Yeshua looked toward heaven. *Father, help me use your power for your glory.* Yeshua knew that just as Yahweh had provided manna in the wilderness during the time of Moses, Yahweh had given him spiritual manna that would give him strength. Turning to Lucifer, he answered, "It is written in the Scriptures: 'One cannot live only on bread but by God's Word.'"

For a moment, Lucifer stepped back as divinity shone through Yeshua's countenance, but not for long. He had been planning this masterful deception for forty days, and he was not ready to give up.

Gabriel and the angels with him followed as Lucifer took Yeshua to the highest point of the temple. Yahweh and El-Shaddai stayed close by.

Lucifer tried again. "If you are really the Son of God, prove it by showing your trust in

The Mission Begins

God's Word by jumping off this building. After all, the Scripture says, 'God will send his angels to take care of you. Even when you fall, they will catch you and keep your foot from hitting a rock on the ground.'"

Once again Yeshua looked toward heaven, *Yahweh, give me your strength so I may reveal your truth.* Knowing that Yahweh's angels come to those whose faith finds refuge in him, Yeshua looked at Lucifer squarely and spoke, "Remember that the Scriptures also say, 'You are not to test God'; therefore, you should not be testing me."

Lucifer cringed at Yeshua's boldness. In anger he tried again. By this point, his light had faded, and the darkness of his true character shone through. Once again, Yahweh and El-Shaddai stayed close to Yeshua as he and Lucifer now stood at the top of a high mountain. Holy angels stood nearby with swords of light sheathed but ready if needed.

They watched as Lucifer showed Yeshua the beautiful kingdoms of the world, their wealth, prestige, and power. "You came here to save the world. That is the hard way. I will show you the easy way. Just bow down to me and give me the honor and worship I deserve. Then, since I own the world, I will give it to you."

Yahweh, Yeshua cried, *you own the world. You are God. Give me your strength to accomplish the mission according to your plan.* Divinity flashed through Yeshua. This time his voice rang with the same authority he had when he had cast Lucifer out of heaven many millennia before. "Get out of here! You have no claim here on earth. The Scriptures clearly say, 'You must only worship the Lord your God and only serve him.'"

Lucifer trembled at Yeshua's words. He saw an army of holy angels standing with their swords of light drawn ready for battle. Lucifer knew he had lost. Immediately he and his evil angels fled.

Exhausted, Yeshua fell to the ground. He had witnessed a taste of the great conflict that had begun in heaven. Only this time he had fought the fight in human form, using Yahweh's divine power instead of his own.

Gabriel made himself visible. Gently he helped Yeshua sit up, allowing Yeshua to rest against him. Another angel brought bread and fresh water. Gabriel broke the bread into pieces and helped Yeshua eat the bread and drink the cool water.

Gabriel looked at Yeshua. "This is so difficult. I fought beside you that horrible day in heaven when Lucifer and his followers were thrown out of heaven. Now I am beside you again, but this time …" He could not hide the ache in his voice. "Oh, Yeshua, you have given up so much. Yet the struggle is just beginning. Please have courage. You have won a great victory for heaven today."

Yes, my son, Yahweh spoke. *You have fought well. The great conflict that is before us is fierce, but the victory is ours.*

* * * * *

John the Baptist spoke to two of his followers. "Remember the Anointed One whom I baptized? I saw him yesterday."

"Yes," Andrew replied enthusiastically, "he is the one on whom God's Spirit rested."

"He is the Messiah," John the Baptist continued. "These last forty days I have been studying the prophecies. While I do not understand everything completely, I am even more convinced that the Anointed One must be both lamb and king. I am not sure how it all fits together yet. I just know it does."

El-Shaddai moved close to John the Baptist. *Look up*, he said gently.

As John the Baptist looked up, he saw Yeshua walking slowly among the people. "There he is. He is the one I told you about. He is the Lamb of God!"

Andrew looked at his friend, another of John the Baptist's followers, whose name was also John. "We want to know more," Andrew said.

"Go," John the Baptist said. "You have my blessing."

Andrew and his friend John ran to catch up to where Yeshua was walking on the road toward Bethany.

El-Shaddai whispered into Yeshua's ear. *You have company. They are eagerly seeking truth.*

Yeshua turned around, waiting for the two men to catch up. "What can I do for you?"

The two friends stopped in front of Yeshua and caught their breath. Andrew then spoke. "Great teacher, where are you staying? John the Baptist talked about the Messiah being a lamb. We would like to learn more and only you can teach us."

Yeshua smiled warmly. "I would love to spend the day with you. We can share a meal together while we talk."

Yahweh grinned. Turning to El-Shaddai, he spoke, *They are so open, so willing to follow. I know Yeshua will teach them well.*

* * * * *

Andrew burst through the door of the house where he was staying with his brother Simon. "Simon, you will not believe what happened today! John, the son of Zebedee, and I were down by the Jordan River talking with John the Baptist, when he pointed out the Anointed One whom he had baptized."

"Really? The Messiah?" Simon leaned against the doorway.

"Yes," Andrew continued, "but there's more. John and I followed him, and he invited us to eat with him. While we ate, he shared with us the prophecies from the great prophet Isaiah. He explained them in a clearer way than anyone has ever before. It was as if he had written them himself."

Andrew grabbed Simon's shoulders, looking intently into his face. "I know he is the Messiah. You've got to meet him. Will you come with me tomorrow?"

Simon grinned, "Andrew, I would love to."

The brothers talked well into the night before finally falling asleep.

* * * * *

Yeshua walked along the pathway toward the house where he was staying. He had already spent the early morning with Yahweh and El-Shaddai, sharing the events of the previous day.

I really enjoyed spending time with John and Andrew, Yeshua told Yahweh and El-Shaddai.

John is young, yet moldable, and eager to learn. He is already beginning to understand the magnitude of your love. He has a deep understanding of spiritual things and has already begun listening to your voice, Yeshua shared enthusiastically. *He will become a great leader.*

Yeshua smiled and continued. *Andrew is one who assesses everything, formulates an opinion, and then acts with conviction.*

Oh yes, Yahweh agreed. *In fact, he and his brother Simon are already on their way to meet you.*

Yeshua laughed, *I can hardly wait.*

El-Shaddai grinned. *You won't be waiting long.*

As Yeshua walked across the courtyard to the house where he was staying, he saw two young men approaching him. Yeshua greeted them warmly. "Good morning!" He nodded toward Andrew. "It is so nice to see you again."

Andrew smiled and said, "This is my brother, Simon."

"Simon," Yeshua mused. His eyes seemed to look into Simon's very soul. "Your name means 'he has heard.' God will always hear your prayers, but he has a special calling for you. To reflect that calling, I am changing your name to Peter."

It was common for rabbis to give new names to their disciples, but Rock was an unusual name. Simon didn't know anyone called that. "Tell me, Master, the significance of the name."

Yeshua looked deeply into Simon's eyes. "You are like a rock. There are times when you may not be steady, like a rock that rolls. But when you understand all things, you will become like a solid rock that cannot be moved."

"Thank you, Master," Simon Peter said. "I would like to become like that rock."

"You will," Yeshua responded as he motioned for the two men to join him under the shade of a nearby tree. "Now tell me what is on your heart …"

* * * * *

As Yeshua walked on the path toward Galilee, Yahweh spoke. *I have thoroughly enjoyed watching you these last few days.*

So have I, El-Shaddai added.

Peter is quite outspoken, Yeshua commented.

Yahweh laughed. *Yes, but when he is changed by El-Shaddai, he will become bold about sharing the Word, and no one will be able to keep him quiet.*

Yeshua grinned. *I love the way you take human traits and transform them for divine use.*

Speaking of which …" El-Shaddai nudged Yeshua toward a man who was giving directions to some travelers who seemed to be lost.

As Yeshua listened, he noticed that the man was speaking fluently in Greek. *He will be a great missionary one day,* he commented to El-Shaddai.

Yeshua waited quietly until the travelers were on their way down the road. As the man started on the path toward Galilee, Yeshua joined him and struck up a conversation.

"Hello, my name is Yeshua. May I travel with you?"

"Yes, my name is Philip," the man told Yeshua.

As they walked, they talked about their families and where they grew up. Then Yeshua began to ask Philip about current events, the teachings of John the Baptist, and the coming Messiah. Philip told him that he had listened to John and wanted to study more. "I want to follow the Messiah," Philip said.

Yeshua looked into Philip's eyes. Seeing his readiness to obey, Yeshua spoke, "I am the one John the Baptist spoke of. Would you like to study with me and become one of my followers?"

"You have chosen me?" Philip paused in the middle of the path. "Oh yes, Master, my greatest desire is to follow you."

Yeshua put his hand on Philip's shoulder. "Then you shall have your heart's desire."

As the two continued walking, El-Shaddai moved close to Philip. Already he was listening to the Spirit's voice. "Master," he suddenly spoke, "I have a friend who is looking for the Messiah also. He has been studying the Scriptures and the laws of Moses. I want him to meet you. You could help him understand everything."

A knowing smile spread across Yeshua's face. "Philip, you are already a missionary. By all means, go find your friend."

"Where will I find you?"

Yeshua noticed a small group of trees close by. "Right over there. I am not in a hurry. I will be more than happy to wait for you."

* * * * *

Nathanael sat quietly under the fig tree near his home where he often went to pray.

He had been at the Jordan River when John the Baptist pointed out the Anointed One as the Lamb of God. Ever since that day he had pondered what John meant. How could the Messiah be a lamb instead of a king? In search of answers, he had spent time studying the prophecies.

Lord, he began, *I need to understand. Please, show me a sign. I need to know for sure who is your Chosen One.*

El-Shaddai whispered to Nathanael. *I will give you a sign. Just keep trusting.*

A twig snapped nearby. Nathanael looked up to find Philip standing beside him.

"Nathanael Bartholomew, I thought I would find you here," Philip said. "I have good news to share with you."

Nathanael looked up at his friend. "Do you have an answer to my prayer?"

Philip sat down beside Nathanael. "Oh yes! I met the Messiah today. He is the one you have been studying about in the Torah and the prophetic Scriptures."

"Really? Who is he?" Nathanael grabbed Philip's arm.

"He is Yeshua of Nazareth. He is the son of Joseph the carpenter," Philip answered. "He told me about his family as we were walking."

"What?" Nathanael looked disgustedly into his friend's face. "People from Nazareth are a poorer class and not as pious as those from Jerusalem! How can the Messiah, who is good, come out of Nazareth?"

Philip stood up and shook his head. "Nathanael, you just need to meet him. He can tell you everything you want to know." He reached out and grabbed Nathanael's hand.

"All right." Nathanael let Philip pull him up. "I will go."

* * * * *

Yeshua did not mind the wait. It gave him time to talk with Yahweh and El-Shaddai. As they were talking, Yeshua looked up and saw Philip with his friend Nathanael coming down the road.

El-Shaddai spoke, *The one with Philip has asked for a sign. He has been praying and studying. He wants to know the truth about the Messiah.* Previously, El-Shaddai had shone Yeshua a vision of Nathanael praying under the fig tree and heard his prayer.

He is one who weighs everything carefully because he wants to put himself completely into whatever he believes, Yeshua observed.

Yahweh agreed. *He will become a great worker, never swerving in his faith.*

Yeshua stood up and began walking toward the two men.

"I am so glad to see you. You are a discerning Israelite whose greatest desire is to know the truth."

Nathanael stared in disbelief. "We have never met before. How do you know me?"

As Yeshua looked lovingly into Nathanael's eyes, divinity shone through. "Before Philip found you, I was shown that you were under a fig tree earnestly praying for truth."

"Oh, Master," exclaimed Nathanael, "you are the Messiah. You are the one who will fulfill all prophecies."

Yeshua put his hand on Nathanael. "Your prayer was answered. All it took was a simple sign for you to believe. Even the Holy Spirit's proclamation during my baptism is small compared to that which will be available to you. Angels will carry your prayers to heaven and bring you answers to all your questions. And when all is fulfilled, you will do great miracles in God's name."

El-Shaddai smiled at Yahweh. "His faith is like a mustard seed."

"Yes," Yahweh grinned. "And I can already see it growing into a tree."

* * * * *

The sun peeked just over the horizon. Its pink, orange, and yellow rays seemed to stretch lazily toward the sky as if the sun was debating as to whether it wanted to get up that morning. "The sunrise you sent this morning is breathtaking," Yeshua said. He had been talking with Yahweh and El-Shaddai well before the sun began to rise.

Thank you, Yahweh said, grinning. *I enjoy spending the time watching it with you.*

Yeshua rested against a small tree. "Of all the sunrises you've fashioned, which one has been your favorite?"

Yahweh laughed. *There are so many—* He paused, recalling memories. *However, it is not the sunrise, but the one who enjoys it with me that makes my heart sing the most.*

Yeshua smiled. He felt Yahweh and El-Shaddai's presence as he spent time talking with them. Watching the sunrise, Yeshua began to sing a song of praise. After the sunrise faded and the sun took its place above the hills, Yeshua stood up and brushed the dust and bits of bark off his tunic. With renewed strength, he walked down the hill toward Cana.

As he approached a large housing complex, Yeshua noticed wedding guests gathered in groups talking and laughing. The wedding had gone well so far. The bridegroom had met with the bride's parents, paid a handsome dowry, and had built a room off his father's house for them to live. The wedding procession had been magnificent, the marriage contract had been signed, and the marriage had been sealed that night. The feasts of celebration had continued for several days now.

Contemplating his mission, Yeshua spoke softly, "Father, your people are the bride. I am the bridegroom. Give me strength to pay the price of the dowry."

"There you are, Master," a familiar voice said. Yeshua saw his new friends coming toward him. They had all been invited to the wedding celebration. "Your mother is looking for you," John announced, pointing to an area near the kitchen. Yeshua nodded and walked toward where John had pointed. He quietly stepped into the corridor where Mary waited. His followers stood close by, as did a handful of servants.

Mary placed her hand on Yeshua's arm. "There are so many more guests here than we had on the original guest list," she began. "Isaac and his family have been our close friends for years." Yeshua leaned forward, listening intently. "I do not know how it happened," she continued, " but the wine was supposed to last seven days, and yet we have run out. You know that weddings must overflow with wine to show God's blessing on his people. Without any wine—" Mary paused. "Yeshua, please help restore honor to Isaac and his family."

Yeshua sighed. "Mother, why are you involving me? You know I can only do miracles if God wants me to do them." Seeing the desperation in his mother's eyes, Yeshua looked to heaven. *Yahweh, you have asked that we honor our earthly parents, but you have also asked that we honor you, our heavenly Father. What would you like me to do?*

Yahweh smiled. *You may honor both.*

Yeshua looked into his mother's eyes and nodded. Mary smiled. She turned to the waiting servants and said, "Do whatever he tells you to do."

Yeshua looked down the corridor. Six large empty jars were lined up against the wall. "Fill those jars with water. Fill them all the way to the top." Yeshua's followers watched as the servants took several trips to the nearby well with smaller jars that they poured into the bigger ones. Yeshua watched amused as his followers discussed what they thought he was going to do with the water. Finally one of the servants came to Yeshua and said, "Master, we have filled the jars with water."

Yeshua nodded. "You have done well. Now, dip a cup in and take some to the master of the banquet. It is his job to make sure there is plenty of good wine for the celebration."

The servant looked at Yeshua in disbelief. He wanted to say something about there only being water in the jars and how that would destroy honor to Isaac and his family, but instead, he only nodded. A servant was not to question a master's orders. Obediently he dipped a cup into one of the jars and filled it with water. The servants stopped serving. The disciples stopped talking. All eyes watched as the servant carefully carried the cup to the master of the banquet.

"Humans are a mystery me," Gabriel said as he drew close to where Yahweh and El-Shaddai were standing. "They have such little faith."

"True," El-Shaddai replied. "But that faith is about to be strengthened."

Everyone watched as the servant handed the cup of water to the master of the banquet. "Here, sir, please taste this and see if it meets your standards."

The man took the cup, closed his eyes, and took a sip. Then he took another sip. He handed the cup to the waiting servant. "That wine is amazing. By all means, serve it to our guests."

Puzzled, the servant looked into the cup. Instead of water, it was filled with a pure red liquid that resembled wine.

"Well," the master of the banquet said, "why are you still standing there? Go and serve the wine. Everyone will want some."

The servant mumbled, "Yes, sir," and hurried back to the waiting group. The servants and disciples gathered around as he showed them the cup that was now filled with wine. They all tasted some and agreed it was the best they had ever tasted.

Gabriel grinned at the small group dancing in the corridor. "Look at how excited they are. It was such a simple miracle, turning water into wine."

Yahweh laughed. "If that seems amazing, just think of what they would do if I showed them how I made the grapes."

While the servants went to serve the wine, Mary came to Yeshua. "Thank you, Yeshua," she said. "You have preserved honor today."

Yeshua hugged her gently. "It was the Father's will."

"I know." She held him tightly. "I am glad it was."

As Mary went back to her duties, Yeshua watched his followers.

"Truly he is the Anointed One," John said in awe.

"Yes," Andrew agreed. "Today has given me courage and hope."

Yeshua looked up toward heaven. *Thank you, Father. Thank you for caring about little details. It has strengthened the faith of those whom you have chosen.*

Yahweh smiled. *It will be one of the miracles that will help keep their faith alive when it is tested most.*

Chapter 5

The Mission of God's Kingdom

Yeshua leaned against a fig tree near the temple wall. It was evening, and the air was growing cooler as the sun settled behind the hills for the night. As the crowds dispersed, those who had been healed reveled in their new beginnings even though the day was ending. Those unable to walk now joyously ran through the marketplace toward their homes. The blind stared in amazement at the beautiful colors of the sunset. The deaf listened intently as children retold the stories they had heard from the Great Rabbi.

Their excitement is contagious. Yahweh whispered to his son.

Yeshua nodded. *It was wonderful when that deaf man started singing 'Alleluias' because he was so elated he could hear.*

El-Shaddai laughed. *Nobody had ever heard him talk before, and there he was singing at the top of his lungs as he walked through the crowd.*

I noticed a Pharisee watching today, Yeshua ventured. *His robe indicated that he is from the Sanhedrin.*

He is, Yahweh commented. *Nicodemus tried to talk with you several times, but there were too many people.*

That is why I thought I would wait here. Yeshua pulled a ripe fig from the tree and placed it in his mouth. *I believe he passes this way each evening.*

He is almost here, El-Shaddai said. *Like the others, he is looking for healing. What he needs is spiritual healing.*

A small door opened as a well-dressed Pharisee walked toward Yeshua. As the man passed the fig tree, Yeshua stepped out and began walking beside him.

Nicodemus turned and looked into Yeshua's face. "Great Teacher, I have been wanting to talk with you. Are you busy?"

"My time is yours." Yeshua smiled, motioning for Nicodemus to join him on a grassy spot not too far down the path.

Nicodemus began what must have been his prepared speech. "We all know you are chosen by God to teach us. God's Spirit is definitely with you." He paused. "I have watched you healing people all day. I want to know more about who you are and what you teach about the kingdom of God."

Yeshua looked into Nicodemus' eyes, but they seemed to read his heart. "Nicodemus, you have seen many people healed today of their diseases and handicaps. They were given a new life. I want you to have a new life too."

Yeshua put his hand on Nicodemus' shoulder. "The only way you will understand the kingdom of God is by being born again."

Nicodemus furrowed his brow. "I do not understand. I am old. Are you saying I need to be born as a baby all over again?"

Yeshua shook his head. "I am not talking about healing your physical body or you being born of your mother so you are young again. I am talking about a new heart and character, a spiritual transformation that makes you a new person—one that can be part of God's kingdom."

Yeshua felt El-Shaddai's presence drawing closer to Nicodemus. "You can only be part of God's kingdom if you are baptized and receive God's Spirit. The Spirit of God is like the wind. He cannot be controlled or manipulated by people. You may not even feel that he is working in you right now. However, you can see the results of his presence by the miraculous changes in your life. These changes will be as dramatic as the miracles you saw today."

Nicodemus looked into Yeshua's eyes. "I am a religious leader. I work in God's temple. I help God's people. I spend my life doing good deeds. How is it that I need a new spiritual life?"

Yeshua smiled. Gently he spoke. "Nicodemus, let me see if I can explain this in a way you can understand. It is not all the good things you do that saves you. You know the story about when God's people were in the wilderness and were bitten by snakes. God told Moses to make a bronze serpent. When it was raised up, all those who saw it were healed. But the bronze snake was not the one who saved them—it was God. Today God's people are still bitten by the serpent called Lucifer. They need to be healed of their sins. This is why I have come. I will be lifted up so that everyone, no matter what religion or race, will be saved if they believe."

El-Shaddai pressed close, speaking to Nicodemus' heart. Nicodemus would become a true believer in the Sanhedrin, at Yeshua's burial, and later in the group of followers who would lead the Christian church. Yeshua continued. "You know Plato's Allegory of the Cave. People are born in the darkness of the cave. Many stay in the darkness forever. Some chose to step out of the cave and follow the light. I am the Light of the world. Look to me. Let me heal you and give you a new life."

Nicodemus sat very quietly as Yeshua's words lingered in his mind. "Master, heal me," he said softly.

Yeshua placed both hands on Nicodemus' shoulders. "Nicodemus, your new life will have many challenges, but you will be strong. You will do great things for me and for those who are part of God's kingdom."

"Thank you, Master," Nicodemus said as he rose to leave.

"Have peace, Nicodemus," Yeshua spoke gently. "God's Spirit will be with you."

As Nicodemus made his way down the path toward his home, Yeshua once again leaned against the fig tree near the temple wall. "I can hardly wait until the earth is healed and all things are new."

Yes, Yahweh agreed. *Just think of all the amazing things we will be able to share with Nicodemus then.*

* * * * *

Yeshua watched as his followers walked down the road that entered the Samaritan village of Sychar. They were on their way to buy food and drink. Judas was carrying the money pouch. Peter, on the other hand, was carrying a container made of animal skins that travelers used to carry water.

Sitting close to the limestone ledge by the well outside the city wall, Yeshua waited for the group to return. He was thirsty, but he knew he would never be able to get water from the well, which was at least one hundred feet deep. However, what he was waiting for was even more important than a drink of water.

As he sat resting, El-Shaddai spoke to his heart. *A woman will soon approach the well to draw water. I have been preparing her to be receptive to what will happen here. Her last few days have been difficult. She is feeling empty and discouraged, longing for something more. Of course, you have something more.*

"There she is now," Yahweh spoke with an eagerness in His voice, for he already anticipated adding another person to become part of the kingdom.

Not expecting to find anyone getting water at noon, the woman tied her jar to the rope, lowered it into the well, and, after hearing a splash and gurgling noise, began pulling it back up. She was so intent on getting her water quickly that she did not realize she was being watched.

"Please," Yeshua began softly, "I am thirsty. May I have a drink?"

The woman spun around to face the one who had spoken. She saw that it was not only a man, but also a Jew. Terrified, she placed her jar onto the ledge and backed away. She was used to men, prejudice, and rejection.

She spoke rudely. "Sir, why are you asking me for a drink? You are a Jew. I am a Samaritan. Jews think we are unclean. Even this water would be unfit to drink for Jews."

Yeshua smiled. "This water is from Jacob's well, which is fed by an underground spring.

We desert dwellers call such water the 'gift of God.'" Yeshua looked straight into her eyes and down into her heart. He felt the longing of her soul, so he offered to give her something that would change her life—the Water of Life. "If only you knew about the true gift of God, you would be asking me to give you a drink, and I would give you living water."

The woman looked skeptically at this strange man. "Sir, you are traveling and did not bring a skin container. How can you draw water? Where is this living water? Are you greater than Jacob, our father, who gave us this well in the first place?"

Yeshua pointed to the well. "Without the underground spring, this well would be empty. Every day you must come here for water, because you use up the water you have drawn and grow thirsty again. Your life is empty like this well would be without the spring. I want to put a spring inside you that will fill you and give you eternal life."

If only I did not have to come here, she thought to herself, *I would not have to contend with the shame and ridicule the village places on me.* Looking into Yeshua's face, she said, "Sir, that would help me so much. Please give me this water so that I do not have to come to the well."

Yeshua saw the hurt she was not expressing and said, "Go and bring your husband."

The woman looked down at the ground, her toe tracing small circles in the sand. Marriages were arranged. She had been married all right. Many times. Men had the right to divorce women they did not like. Somehow, she was disliked, hated, beaten. She was bought and sold like an animal. The man she was with now did not even bother to marry her. That meant he did not have to take care of her. She might as well have been a slave. She sighed. Not even looking up, she spoke, "I do not have a husband."

El-Shaddai pressed closed to Yeshua, sharing with him her thoughts and her life of rejection and pain. "What you say is true," Yeshua spoke gently. "You have had five husbands, and you are not married to the man you are living with now."

The woman shrank back. How could this man know her painful past? She did not want him to go any deeper. It hurt too much to talk about it. "Sir, you must be a prophet to know what I have not yet told you." She paused, changing the subject. "So tell me, you Jews say Jerusalem is the place to worship. We Samaritans say Mount Gerizim is the place to worship. Which is right?" A smirk spread across the woman's face. Debates of philosophy or religion were common, and she was good at defending herself. She had to in order to survive.

Yeshua sighed. A jar filled with contempt, sin, and pride could never be filled with the Living Water. As El-Shaddai sought to soften the woman's heart, Yeshua continued to clean the dirty jar of her life.

"My dear woman," Yeshua began gently as he looked into the future and saw the Romans under Titus destroying Jerusalem, "you are missing the point. There will be a time in the future when both temples will be destroyed. However, the important thing is not where you worship, but whom you worship. Your people only have part of the truth. You have mixed pagan ideals with the truth. The Jews have the truth, and a time is soon coming when they will share that salvation with non-Jews. God is spirit. Therefore, if you want to worship the true God, you must worship him, not with outward rituals, but in spirit and truth with your whole heart. His truth must become real inside you."

The woman looked at Yeshua. This man was different. He looked at her, not to use her, but to change her. "Sir, it seems you want to change my life into something better. We Samaritans believe in a Messiah who will teach us the truth."

A smile spread across Yeshua's face. "I am the Messiah, the Anointed One."

"Oh!" the women cried. "I must tell my people! The one we have longed for is here." Leaving her jar, she ran down the road back into the city.

Yahweh laughed. *She left her jar of water.*

True, Yeshua observed, *but the spring inside her is already overflowing to those who are thirsty.*

El-Shaddai grinned. *Yes, and many will be filled today.*

* * * * *

The mountainside was covered with people sitting around Yeshua as he spoke. His followers sat close by him. With authority and power, Yeshua shared with them the truths of the kingdom of God. Unseen by the people, El-Shaddai circulated his presence around those listening, touching all who were willing and ready to be transformed.

"I love to hear him preach," Gabriel sighed contentedly. "Even if it is simplified for humans, the truths are so powerful."

"Yes," Yahweh grinned. "I am so excited by the many hearts that are responding to El-Shaddai's promptings and accepting the message."

Yeshua's rich voice fell on every listening ear. "Do you want a kingdom of peace? Then you must seek God's kingdom. If you want to know God's peace, you must realize you are nothing without God. Do you have sorrow in your heart? Let God's peace comfort you. Do you want to have a great reward in God's kingdom? Be humble and let God lift you up. Do you hunger for justice? Be content for God's judgment. Do you want to experience God's generosity? Be generous to others. Do you want to see God? Then keep your hearts pure. Do you want to be children of God? Then work for peace, not strife. Do you feel persecuted for doing right? Let God's peace give you courage."

As Yeshua spoke, a man stood off by himself. His clothes were torn. A cloth covered the lower half of his face. Scattered white patches covered his dirty skin. Tears filled his eyes. He wanted peace. He wanted to be part of God's kingdom, but his own people had rejected him. He was told God had rejected him too, and cursed with this dreaded leprosy.

El-Shaddai wrapped his arms around the stricken man. Willingness to be healed would need faith, and faith, action. As if reading the man's thoughts, Yeshua continued. "Is your greatest desire to be a part of God's kingdom? Then keep asking, and you will receive. Keep seeking, and you will find what you are looking for. Keep knocking, and the door of opportunity will be opened. Your heavenly Father is eager to give good gifts to you, his child."

You are God's child, El-Shaddai whispered to the leper's heart.

I have been cast out, the leper argued in his own mind.

Even a cast out child is still his child. Go—ask, seek, and knock, El-Shaddai countered.

I might be rejected, again, the man thought, putting his head in his gnarled hands. *Oh how I long to be well. I want to be included in God's kingdom.* He straightened his body to his full height. Determined, the man fixed his eyes on the Great Healer. "Unclean!" he called.

The crowd parted as he made his way toward the top of the mountain. People shouted. "Get out of here!" One man threw a small stone at him. "Go back to where you belong. Do not contaminate others."

Resolutely, the leper continued his quest, ignoring the fearful and hateful cries of the people. At last he reached the top of the mountain where he knelt at Yeshua's feet.

"I know you are from God. You have power to heal anyone. But I am condemned. I have leprosy." Tears ran down the man's face. "If … if …" the man paused. "If you are willing, you can heal me of this disease. You can make me clean so that I am part of God's kingdom." The leper cowered, waiting for the words of condemnation he had heard so many times before.

Yeshua had seen how the people had treated this leper. With tenderness, he placed his hands on the leper's shoulders. Startled, the leper looked into Yeshua's face. It had been so long since he had been touched. The warmth of those strong hands wrapped around his heart, melting away the pain and rejection. He wanted to stay there forever. Yeshua's gentle eyes looked into the man's eyes. "I am willing. You are healed."

El-Shaddai's presence enveloped the leper. A surge of energy cascaded through the man's body. His gnarled hands straightened. The white patches morphed into healthy skin. His despair disintegrated into peace.

Yeshua's strong hands helped the man to his feet. "Welcome to God's kingdom. God has already claimed you as his. Now go show yourself to the priests so God's people can legally accept you, giving you the right to rejoin your family."

"Yes, sir," the man said gripping Yeshua's hands tightly. He did not want to ever forget what they felt like. Reluctantly he let go. Then he turned and ran down the mountain path toward the village.

The crowd dispersed. People talked about the miraculous healing of the man whom they did not think God could love and forgive. As he watched the people leave, Yeshua whispered softly. *They have so many misconceptions of you. They do not understand that your love is unconditional.*

Human love is shallow. They cannot comprehend infinite love, El-Shaddai added.

That is why you are Immanuel, God with them, Yahweh added. *When they see your love, they will feel my love. Then our love will be real to them.*

* * * * *

John sat beside Yeshua in a quiet corner in Peter's family's courtyard where they were staying. He did not want to disturb the Master, but there were so many people. "Master, if you are ready, there are many people here to see you."

"Do not worry, John," Yeshua put his hand on John's shoulder. "If people are truly seeking, then I am available."

John rose to his feet. "Then I will tell the people they can come in the house." As John went to help Peter prepare the house for a large meeting, Yeshua lingered.

It is a mixed multitude, El-Shaddai noted. *Some come to learn, others to debate. Some wish to be healed, others think they already are.*

Yahweh agreed. *A mixed multitude brings mixed blessings.*

Then I will need your wisdom, Father, Yeshua spoke softly as he rose to his feet and slowly walked into the house.

Peter had arranged for Yeshua to stand at the front of the large room. The walls of the house were made of basalt stones placed together with mud and small stones. The thatched roof was made of wooden beams made from tree branches that rested over the top of the walls. The roof was overlaid with mud, reeds, and palm branches. The sun's light came from a small window and the open door, both of which were blocked by people. As Yeshua shared stories about God's kingdom, people continued to crowd into the house until there was no more room. Yeshua spoke loudly so those standing outside could hear as well.

Seemingly unnoticed, four men approached the house. They were carrying a thin mat stuffed with straw. On it was a man who lay in a spastic rigor that twisted his body into an unnatural position. Drool dripped from his mouth into a small pool on the mat. His eyes stared as if unseeing into the faces of his friends.

"Look at the crowd," the tallest man spoke. "It looks impossible to get in." Several times the four men tried to push through, but it was no use.

"There has to be a way," one of the younger man countered. "It is our only hope. He does not have much time left."

The tall man nodded, "I know. We must find a way."

Thoughtfully, the oldest man spoke. "Let us go around to those stairs leading to the roof. Maybe …"

The men walked around the crowd to the back stairs that led to the roof. With two pulling the mat up the stairs and two guiding from behind, they managed to get the palsied man onto the roof. As they paused to rest, the men listened. They could hear Yeshua speaking below them in the house.

"The Great Healer's voice is loudest here." The youngest man stood by a spot near the back of the house. "This is where he is."

Placing the mat securely on the roof, the three men joined the younger man. They dug through the turf, removing the reeds and palm branches. Carefully they spread the beams apart until the hole was large enough for the mat to fit through. Then they lowered their friend until he rested safely at Yeshua's feet.

The palsied man's seemingly unseeing eyes stared upward. He tried to focus. His body hardly worked. His mind seemed to be in a dark fog. The priests had told him that God had cursed him because of his terrible sins. Even the doctors said there was no cure. The disease had spread, crippling not only his body but also his hope. Knowing he would die forgotten, with no life to come, shrouded his soul. Depression darkened his world, shrinking it until there seemed to be nothing left.

Yeshua looked up into the faces of the four brave men. These men had not given up on their friend. They had taken turns caring for him. They had offered sacrifices for his sins. They had prayed on his behalf. Now hope had kindled a fire in their hearts. With unswerving faith they had brought him to Yeshua to be healed. Not even difficult circumstances and obstacles had stopped them. They had done for their friend what he could not do for himself. Their faith was about to be richly rewarded.

Yeshua gave a reassuring nod to the four waiting friends. Then he turned to the man on the mat. Answering the longing of the poor man's soul, Yeshua spoke with authority. "My child, your sins are forgiven."

As Yeshua spoke, the palsied man's unseeing eyes began to focus. Light began to dissipate his darkness. His mind became clear. Peace filled his soul. He knew now that he could die, forgiven.

The same words that had brought peace to the palsied man sparked dissention in others. Though they said nothing, some of the teachers of the law were greatly offended. This act of blasphemy was worthy of death.

As El-Shaddai revealed their thoughts to Yeshua, he responded with authority. "You know that Moses states that if a prophet speaks in God's authority and it does not come true the prophet is false. Let me then show you proof for your doubts. If this man is healed, then it validates that I have both the power to forgive sins and to heal."

Turning to the man on the mat, Yeshua spoke. "Son, stand up! You are healed. Pick up your mat and go home."

Immediately a healing power encircled the palsied man. His rigid body relaxed. His gnarled limbs straightened. Energy surged through his soul. Yeshua grinned and took the man's hands, helping him to his feet. The palsied man looked around at his surroundings.

A deafening applause from above caught his attention. He looked up into the grinning faces of his four best friends. Yeshua pointed upward. "I think they are waiting for you."

"Yes, they are. Thank you, sir!" The man grabbed his mat and walked proudly through the stunned crowd. A few minutes later shouts of joy reverberated through the house as the five friends reunited.

After the crowd had dispersed, Yeshua found his way back to the secluded place in the courtyard to sit and reflect on the events of the day.

It was a good day, El-Shaddai mused.

Yahweh nodded. *Some learned, some debated, and some were healed.*

Yeshua sat thoughtfully. *That man who was healed is truly blessed. His friends never gave up.*

Humans may never know how much their faith and prayers will save someone they love. But today those four man saw their hope become a reality, Yahweh said.

Hearing men talking, Yeshua turned to see Peter coming toward him. Yeshua continued the conversation as he stood up. *I promised Peter I would help him with his roof.* And the Three laughed.

Chapter 6

Mission of Hope

Yeshua had once again spent the night in prayer, sharing his thoughts about different aspects of his mission and seeking guidance as to the right course to follow. A part of his mission on earth included training those who could be an extension of his work and could carry the church forward after he left earth. Just as there were twelve tribes of Israel, so there were to be twelve apostles, or messengers. As the sun broke over the horizon, the conversation about the selection of disciples continued.

Peter speaks his mind, Yeshua mused.

Yahweh laughed. *His boldness will make him a mighty leader one day, even to the point of death.*

His brother Andrew is in tune with my prompting, El-Shaddai observed. *He is always bringing people to you who are seeking the truth.*

Then there are James and John, Yeshua continued. *They are another set of brothers with tremendous potential, even though they get angry easily.*

Yes, but they are willing to be molded to my desires, El-Shaddai noted.

Yahweh spoke thoughtfully. *Both will stand firm for God. James will be the first to die; John, the last.*

John has a tender heart, Yeshua spoke fondly. *He is the most perceptive to truth.*

El-Shaddai agreed. *He will be given the tremendous task of recording not only the past but also the future.*

Philip is good with languages and has already proven to be an eager missionary, Yeshua shared, recalling his first experience with Philip.

Yahweh grinned. *Wait until he is filled with El-Shaddai's presence.*

El-Shaddai laughed. *I am going to love guiding him from place to place.*

His friend Nathanael is honest, a true student of the Word, Yeshua continued.

He will share that knowledge in mighty ways, El-Shaddai added.

Then there is Thomas, Yahweh suggested. *He is slow to believe, but when his faith takes hold, he is strong.*

Matthew is a faithful follower, Yeshua commented as he thought about the day he had called him. *Matthew was working in his booth collecting taxes when I walked by. He watched me so intently that I knew he wanted to be with me.*

It was so exciting, Yahweh said. *Matthew did not even stop to count his money. He just left his work and followed you.*

Then he threw a banquet, El-Shaddai noted. *He wanted all of his friends to meet you and get to know you.*

Yeshua laughed. *I wonder what Rome would do if all their tax collectors left and became followers of the truth?* Then he continued. *There is also Simon the Zealot. His life must seem so quiet after being a guerilla fighter.*

Yahweh smiled, *Now he wants to fight for the right kingdom.*

Then there are Thaddeus and James, son of Alphaeus, El-Shaddai ventured.

They are sincere and intensely loyal, Yeshua noted. *They bring a sense of stability to the group.*

Before the conversation ended, he sought guidance as to what he should do about Judas. *The others think very highly of him,* Yeshua stated. *He has a lot of potential.*

His life must be completely surrendered in order for us to change him. Without that commitment... Yahweh paused with concern.

Working with me will give him the greatest opportunity for salvation, Yeshua concluded.

I will continue to work on his heart, El-Shaddai promised.

The rest is his choice, Yahweh added. *We never force our will on anyone.*

Yeshua finished his conversation with El-Shaddai and Yahweh about the twelve as the sun began to rise over the mountains. His followers would be awakening soon, so Yeshua slipped back to the camp and waited for everyone to get up; then he called the twelve to come near and kneel before him. He placed his hands on each disciple as he prayed specifically for each one. Motioning for the disciples to stand, Yeshua spoke, "You have been set aside for a special purpose. Going in pairs, you are to carry on my work, preaching that God's kingdom is near. In my name you will be able to cast out demons and heal every disease. Begin in the towns of Israel where we have already been. Do not worry about your needs, for God will provide."

Yeshua continued, offering these words of advice. "I send you out as sheep in a den of wolves. You will need to be wise as snakes, but your demeanor must be as calm and gentle as a dove. As you witness for me now and in the future, you will be brought before kings and governors. You will even be called into the court of synagogues. Do not worry about what you will say for you will be given the words you will need at that time. You will be beaten, persecuted, and even killed. But you will be given the courage you need, and all those who endure to the end will be saved."

A deep awe fell upon the twelve disciples. Quietly they gathered into groups of two. Each pair met with the Master to receive final instructions. Then they set out to complete the work they had been given.

* * * * *

While his followers were gone, Yeshua devoted his time to preaching, teaching, and healing the sick. One day two followers of John the Baptist approached him. "John has sent us to you. Are you the Messiah? Or should we keep looking for someone else?"

Yeshua looked sympathetically at the two men. Their devotion for their master was evident. He also knew that John was discouraged. Herod Antipas had imprisoned him and was holding him captive in his Machaerus fortress. John had spent his life serving God and calling people to repentance in preparation for the coming Messiah.

Yeshua remembered the day they had met at his baptism when El-Shaddai had encircled him in a dovelike form. Yahweh had spoken, proclaiming Yeshua's divinity and mission. This gave John hope, but now he was discouraged. While his followers visited him, they shared great stories of Yeshua's miracles. Yeshua did not seem to be attempting to overthrow the Romans. John began to wonder if he had been wrong about His convictions that Yeshua was the Messiah.

More than anything, Yeshua wanted to climb the rocky mountain, break into the fortress, and encourage John in person. But Yahweh was not directing Yeshua to go comfort John by his presence. Instead, he would give John the information he needed to endure.

Turning to John's followers, Yeshua invited them to spend the day with him. As soon as his presence was known, people began coming to Yeshua. He blessed children, healed the sick, cast out demons. He shared stories about God's kingdom, carefully selecting ones he knew would encourage John. During lulls in activity, Yeshua shared with John's followers Scriptures that told about his true ministry. He also shared enduring promises that would sustain John. As the day drew to a close, Yeshua called the two followers to him one last time.

"Go tell John what you have seen today. Tell him that the blind see, the deaf hear, the lame walk, the lepers are cured, and the dead are raised to life. Tell him the good news is being preached to the poor. Scripture is being fulfilled."

Yeshua continued, "Tell him what you have heard today. Share with him the Scriptures I have shared with you. Give him the promises I have given you. Tell him that God will greatly bless those who will not turn away because of me."

"Thank you," the two responded. "We will tell John your answer."

As the two turned to leave, they stopped for a moment to listen to Yeshua's clear voice as he spoke to the people about John. "When you went to hear John preach, did he waver like a reed in the wind or did he stand strong? Was he dressed in finest clothing or did he wear simple clothes fit for his work? John was indeed a prophet and more. He was given the special task of preparing the way for the Messiah. People have listened to his preaching and the kingdom of heaven has advanced. Others have also violently opposed it. He is the

Elijah who is to come."

Encouraged, John's followers eagerly went on their way to share with John what they had heard and seen.

As the sun disappeared over the horizon, Yeshua climbed a nearby mountain. He was glad his followers were not there. He needed to spend another night in prayer.

I have been thinking about John all day, Yeshua began, resting against a tree.

El-Shaddai spoke, thoughtfully, *I spent the day with him.*

I wish we could intervene, Yeshua sighed. *John completed the work he was called to do.*

Even in prison he is still doing my will, Yahweh pointed out. *Herod Antipas still has choices to make. John's presence will help him make them."*

Taking John's life might stop his preaching, but it cannot stop its message, Yeshua observed.

Yahweh agreed. *In fact, the message will haunt Herod even more.*

There is something else to consider. El-Shaddai paused as he looked into the future. *Many of your followers will die a martyr's death. And many more will follow in their footsteps as history unfolds. John's death will be a comfort to them. Knowing that he stayed true to his conviction even though he never saw the results of his work will help others to stand firm.*

With tears in his eyes, Yahweh sighed. *I cannot take that cup away. As your forerunner, he must taste from the cup of suffering that is ultimately yours.*

There was silence for many minutes until El-Shaddai spoke. *John must drink the cup, but I will be there with Him.*

* * * * *

A short time later John sat in his prison cell listening to the report his followers had brought him of their time with Yeshua. El-Shaddai enveloped his presence around John. As they concluded sharing what they had seen and heard, John said, "He is the Messiah. You must follow him. He will fulfill everything in his time."

John had been filled with El-Shaddai's presence at birth. He had listened to El-Shaddai in the desert. Now, alone John spent his closing hours listening to El-Shaddai speak to his heart. The messianic prophecies became clear. He saw that Yeshua was fulfilling the Scriptures. As time passed, he knew that his own work was completed. Even though he would never see the results of what he had preached, he had not turned away. He had endured to the end—he had been faithful to his calling.

* * * * *

Some time later the disciples rejoined Yeshua, sharing their marvelous experiences they had encountered during their missionary journey. One evening as the sun began to drop below the hills, Yeshua and his followers walked to the base of a mountain near Galilee. As his followers prepared to get some sleep, Yeshua asked Peter, James, and John to accompany him further up the mountain so he could pray.

Finding a secluded spot, the three disciples rested while Yeshua went a little further to talk to Yahweh and El-Shaddai. The news of John's death reminded Yeshua of the suffering that was to come and the future persecution of his followers—Peter would be crucified; James would die by the sword; and John would have to endure persecution and isolation.

Father, Yeshua began, *I need your strength. Help me to be able to accomplish this mission. Also, Father, my followers need you not only in my hour of trial, but also in theirs. Please give them the assurance they need.*

Yahweh drew very close to his son while El-Shaddai enclosed around them. Suddenly the glory of their presence radiated around Yeshua. His divinity overshadowed his humanity. Here, in his first coming, Yeshua came clothed in humanity. Now his divinity showed what he would look like at his second coming. Light radiated from his body. His long robe was white with a gold sash. His head and hair were as white as snow. His eyes blazed like fire, and his legs like bronze. And his face shone as the sun.

Two shining figures approached Yeshua. Moses spoke first, reminiscing with Yeshua about the great exodus of God's people, the wandering in the desert, and the triumph of reaching the Promised Land. Moses shared his disappointment of not being able to cross over with the people, only seeing the land from a distance. Yeshua understood the significance. He, too, would die, but unlike Moses his death would ensure that God's people would reach the promised land—heaven.

Then it was Elijah's turn to speak. They talked about the miracles he performed as a prophet of God, the three and half years of waiting for rain, and the ultimate showdown and God's infinite display of power. They rejoiced as they spoke of the chariot of angels that took Elijah to heaven. Yeshua understood the symbolism here, as well. He preached, taught, and performed miracles. His ministry would be three and half years in a country thirsty for the Water of Life. His death would be the greatest revelation of God's infinite love. His death would also make it possible for people to be translated at His second coming.

As they talked with one another, El-Shaddai gently woke up the sleeping disciples. Amazed at the sight before them, the three drowsy disciples watched in awe and wonder. Any doubt of Yeshua's divinity was erased—he was more than just sent from God, he was God.

Bold as ever, Peter blurted out, "It is so wonderful that you have allowed us to be here. Let us build three memorial tabernacles, one for each of you."

Ignoring Peter's feeble attempt to make sense of all that was happening, El-Shaddai enhanced the moment by configuring his presence into a cloud of light. Then Yahweh spoke, "This is my son, the Anointed One. Listen to him."

Terrified, the three disciples fell to the ground. At that moment, the cloud of light faded away, and the brilliant figures disappeared. Cautiously Peter, James, and John stood up. Yeshua, in his veiled human form, stood alone.

Yeshua smiled at his followers who were still reeling from the event of the last few moments. "You do not have to understand it all now. But when I am raised from the dead, it will become clear. Then you will be able to share it with the others."

As Yeshua and his followers bedded down for the remainder of the night, Yeshua took a few moments to finish his conversation with Yahweh. *Thank you, Father, you answered my prayer in a mighty way.*

Yahweh grinned, *I knew you needed it. And Moses and Elijah could hardly wait to see you.*

Yeshua smiled. *It was good to see them again.*

El-Shaddai laughed. *I was just thinking of Peter. He meant well, but he just does not understand yet.*

Yeshua chuckled. *Yes, but one day it will all make sense to him.*

El-Shaddai agreed. *Then, he will be bold in speaking, living, and dying.*

And James? Yeshua asked.

Oh yes, Yahweh assured. *This encounter will sustain him at the end of his life.*

What about John? Yeshua queried.

John will never forget tonight, El-Shaddai answered. *That image of you being glorified will never leave his mind. In fact, it will become part of his final book.*

Chapter 7

Mission of Power

As the moon began to rise in the sky, Yeshua turned to his followers. "Let us go to the other side of the lake." Without hesitation, the disciples started down the hillside to the Sea of Galilee. As fishermen, they were used to spending the night on a lake. Picking one of the large boats owned by some of his followers, Yeshua climbed in. Peter, Andrew, James, and John grabbed the oars. Nathanael sat by the rudder. Then the rest of the disciples climbed in. Since the boat was designed for a crew of fishermen, it also had a sleeping space under the stern deck so the crew could take shifts.

It had been a long day, and Yeshua was tired. Wrapping a cloak around himself, he lay down with his head on a sandbag and was soon asleep. The boat drifted lazily on the water. Enjoying the evening, the followers talked about the day's events and all that they had learned.

Yahweh and El-Shaddai drew near, watching the breeze move Yeshua's dark brown hair.

"He looks so peaceful," El-Shaddai said quietly.

"Yes," said Gabriel as he joined them. "Yet he is so ..."

"Human?" Yahweh suggested.

Gabriel nodded. "It is just so hard to see the Creator so vulnerable."

"Maybe so," El-Shaddai said, "but he is safe in our hands."

Gabriel looked up, noting the sudden change in the night air. "It looks like his followers will need that safety too."

Near the Sea of Galilee were two large valleys that channeled wind toward the lake. Located more than six hundred feet below sea level, the lake was susceptible to down drafts that would collide with the warm air near the lake, often causing sudden storms to occur.

Being experienced fisherman, the men knew what to do when the storm came up out of nowhere. They quickly adjusted the sails and changed their rowing pattern. However, the winds kept whipping through the air, pulling the water into majestic waves. The waves gained momentum until a seven-foot wave crashed onto the boat. Those who were not rowing were frantically bailing water. This storm was the most severe they had experienced. They knew of men who did not return when storms of this magnitude hit.

Peter started giving orders. Suddenly he realized that one of their crew was missing. "The Master!" he shouted. One of the followers dropped down to where Yeshua was sleeping and frantically shook him. "Master! Is it not important to you that we are going to drown?"

Yeshua awoke—his senses taking in his surroundings. He felt the surge of the waves. He heard the screaming of the wind. He sensed the terror in his followers. But he himself had no fear. Yeshua stood with one hand on the mast of the boat. Facing the raging winds, he raised his other hand upward. The Creator of the universe had spoken, and the world had come into existence. Once again he spoke, commanding nature to obey his will.

Divine power surged through him as his voice resonated above the noise of the storm. "Silence! Peace! Be still!"

Immediately Yahweh stopped the whipping winds and calmed the raging waves. The twelve sat stunned—their terror was replaced by peace and awe.

"Why were you afraid?" Yeshua asked. "Did you forget I was in the boat? Have faith. No matter what storm you face, I am bigger than your storm."

His followers just sat there, amazed. Even Peter was quiet. Yeshua calmly went back to where he had been resting when the storm hit.

"So human?" Yahweh queried.

Gabriel laughed. "I love it when his divinity shines through. It gives humans just a glimpse of who he really is."

El-Shaddai nodded. "They were amazed tonight, but just imagine what they would have done if they could have experienced his full glory."

"True," Yahweh added. "Yet, if they could just grasp what they saw today, they would never be afraid again."

* * * * *

It was morning when Yeshua and his followers reached the other shore. They stepped onto the beach. They were now in non-Jewish territory in the region of the Gerasenes, which was part of ten Greek cities under Roman rule. Burial caves dotted the hillside.

As they walked toward the village, eerie cries emerged from one of the caves. Cringing, the disciples looked up to see what ferocious animals were near. Instead, they saw two men running toward the boat as if they were wild animals intent on tearing them to pieces. The chains that had been used to restrain them were now broken, dangling from their wrists and ankles. Torn, ragged, bloodstained clothes hung haphazardly on their bodies. Their hair was long and matted. Their eyes angrily glared at the new arrivals. No longer looking human, they resembled and acted as the demons that possessed them.

Terror struck the disciples. They ran down the road toward the boat. Looking back, they were surprised to see Yeshua still standing where they left him. Unknown to his followers, Yeshua was not alone. Yahweh stood close by his son while El-Shaddai's presence shown around them. Gabriel stood nearby with several guardian angels waiting for Yeshua's command.

Yeshua raised his hand as the demoniacs approached him. Divine authority resonated in his voice, "Evil spirits, get out of these men!"

Instead of attacking, the two demon-possessed men threw themselves at Yeshua's feet. Speaking through one of the men, the demons shouted. "Yeshua, the Son of God. Why are you here? In the name of the Most High God, please do not torment us before our time!"

Yeshua shook his head. He knew that exorcists felt they could control demons if they knew the demons' names. Now, here, the demons were trying to keep him from casting them out by using God's name to protect themselves. "What is your name?" Yeshua asked, countering their attack.

Still protecting themselves from giving a true name, the demons responded, "My name is Legion, for there are many of us in these men."

Nearby, there was a hillside where many farmers gathered with their pigs. The combined herds had two thousand pigs feeding there. "We want to possess those pigs," the demons begged. "Send us to them."

Yeshua allowed them to invade the pigs. Soon the pigs, which normally never traveled in herds, were stampeding down the bank into the lake. Yeshua knew the two men before him were pagans. In their belief system they would see demons as localized. Therefore, the "land demons" that previously controlled them would be "killed" along with the pigs in the water. Knowing this, the men would not live in constant fear of being possessed again.

By now the two men sat peacefully in front of Yeshua. The storm of their lives had been calmed. The disciples had found extra robes in the boat and gave them to the two men. With their minds now clear, the two men sat quietly listening as Yeshua shared simple truths about God.

Gabriel turned to Yahweh. "The contrast is amazing," he observed. "When people give themselves fully to you, they are given a better life. They even have free choice to continually follow you. They have something to live for now."

Yahweh smiled. Gabriel continued. "But when men are controlled by the evil one, their lives are horrific. Their free choice is taken away, and they no longer have a reason to live, only to die."

El-Shaddai nodded. "That is why Yeshua has come. Humans must be set free from the bondage of sin."

Yahweh agreed. "Even if they do not choose life, at least they have a choice."

Meanwhile, the men who herded the pigs ran to the nearby town. They told everyone they met what had happened. Many people in the town gathered around Yeshua and his followers. They were amazed to see that the two men were healed. Sadly, they were terrified of Yeshua's tremendous power, and they asked him to leave.

As Yeshua and his followers got back in the boat, Yeshua turned to the two men who had been healed. "Go home to your friends and families. Tell them everything the Lord God has done for you. Let them know he is a merciful and loving God."

The two men stood on the bank watching the boat carry Yeshua and his followers far across the lake. "Come," one man said to the other. "We have a story to tell." Eagerly the two men walked up the path toward their home village.

* * * * *

It was mid-morning when Yeshua and his followers arrived on the shore. They were back in Jewish territory, and people gathered around them as they entered the nearby town. The crowd parted as a distinguished man approached Yeshua. Jairus was a leader in the synagogue. Falling at Yeshua's feet, Jairus pleaded. "My only child is dying. Please come and place your hands on her so that she might be healed and live."

Yeshua's heart ached. Having a child was very important in a Jewish home. Losing an only child, even if it was a girl, was considered a tragedy. Placing his hand on the man's shoulder, he spoke softly, "I will."

The crowd followed as Jairus led Yeshua to his house. As they were walking, someone brought a deaf man to Yeshua to be healed. Yeshua stopped, placed his hands on the man's ears, and the man could hear. As they continued down the road, a man carried a small child toward Yeshua. Yeshua placed his hands on the child's forehead, and the fever left him. Further along the path, a young man limped over to Yeshua. Once again, Yeshua stopped to touch the young man's leg, and the young man ran joyfully down the road.

Normally Jairus would have been excited to witness Yeshua's miraculous power in action. But today, however, a nagging worry enveloped him. His daughter was dying. The doctors had told him she did not have much time left. When Yeshua had come to town, Jairus felt a measure of hope, but would they make it in time?

Jairus was not the only person in the crowd with a heavy heart. A woman who had been bleeding for twelve years also longed to be healed by Yeshua. It seemed the bleeding would go on for days, far longer than for other women. When it finally stopped, it would start again before she finished her purification. It was a vicious cycle that never seemed to end.

She sighed. Her condition meant she was always unclean. She could not go to social gatherings or even worship in the temple. Even her family could not touch her things. She stayed in her house, leaving only to get necessities. She tried to get help from doctors. They tried all sorts of bizarre remedies, but she only got worse. Now, for the first time in years, hope filled her heart.

She knew she had to be careful. She could not approach him, for she was unclean. *If only I could touch his robe*, she thought, *I would be well. Maybe I can push my way through the crowd without being detected.* The people jostled and pushed her as she made her way toward Yeshua. Finally, she was close enough that she reached out and touched the blue tassel on the hem of his robe. Instantly she felt a surge through her entire being. Her stomach no longer hurt. Energy flowed through her anemic body. She knew that the blood had stopped flowing out of her. She was finally healed. She sighed with relief.

Yeshua felt his healing power emanate from his body. Turning around, he asked, "Who touched my robe?"

The crowd stopped. Peter looked at Yeshua. "Master, everyone is crowding around you so tightly, how could someone not touch you?"

Yeshua shook his head. "Peter, I did not ask who bumped into me. I asked who touched me and was healed."

By now Yeshua's eyes met with those of the woman. She knew she had broken the law. She had touched a man's robe while she was unclean. Terrified, she fell on her knees and begged for forgiveness. When she finished her story, she cowered, waiting for condemnation. Instead, Yeshua reached down. He touched her chin, raising her face until her eyes met his. "My daughter," he spoke gently, "your faith has healed you. Your suffering is over."

She was overwhelmed. Tears ran down her face. Yeshua gently wiped them away and helped her to her feet. "Thank you," she said. Then she disappeared into the crowd.

The group continued down the road. In the distance they could see a man running toward them. As he drew near, he stopped in front of Jairus. "Do not bother the Master," he said. "It is too late. Your daughter is dead."

Jairus' shoulders dropped. He put his head in his hands. *We were almost there. If the Master had come to my house first, maybe …*

He could not complete the thought. He felt numb from the awful news of his sweet daughter's death. Then Jairus felt a gentle hand on his shoulder, and he heard Yeshua's gentle voice. "Keep trusting. Your daughter will be healed."

Telling the crowd to wait, Yeshua took Peter, James, and John and followed Jairus to his house. The girl's mother led them to the room where the young girl was lying. Yeshua held her lifeless hand. Speaking in Aramaic, Yeshua said, "Talitha koum, little girl, get up."

As Yeshua spoke, Yahweh moved close to Yeshua. El-Shaddai wrapped his presence around the little girl. Divine power surged through Yeshua, and the girl opened her eyes. Yeshua smiled and helped the girl to her feet. "Mother! Father!" she cried. She walked over to them, and they threw their arms around her.

Yeshua knew Jairus was overwhelmed. He wanted to reassure Jairus that his daughter was truly alive and not a ghost. "Do you have something for her to eat?" he asked.

"Oh yes!" the girl's mother exclaimed. She found some leftover bread in a small basket by the girl's mat and brought it to her daughter. "She would not eat it before."

Yeshua grinned. "I am sure she will now."

The hungry girl quickly ate the food her mother gave her. Now Jairus knew Yeshua had answered his request. His daughter was alive.

Looking up, he went to thank Yeshua, but he was already gone.

"Where did the Healer go?" the girl asked.

Jairus smiled. "I am sure he has already joined the crowd, so he can heal someone else who has been waiting."

* * * * *

The early morning sun rested on the crowd of people who had gathered around Yeshua and his followers. They were so engrossed in the story Yeshua was telling that they hardly noticed a young boy searching for a vacant place to sit. Finding a suitable spot near the front, he placed the basket containing his lunch down in front of him and began to listen. As Yeshua spoke, he looked at each individual listening as if each person was the only one there.

It was late in the afternoon when the sun dipped down in the western sky. The young lad was so engrossed in the stories Yeshua told that he had forgotten all about his lunch.

Nearby Philip and Andrew were discussing the lateness of the hour. They were hungry and figured the people were too.

Hearing the discussion, Yeshua turned to Philip. "You are from this area. Do you know where we can get enough bread to feed everyone?"

Philip shook his head, "Master, we are in a remote place. Even if there were small shops, we do not have enough money. It would take more than eight months' salary to pay for enough food. The situation seems impossible."

Meanwhile, Andrew looked around the crowd. He noticed a young lad sitting toward the front with a small basket lying beside him. Andrew approached the boy and pointed to the basket. "Is this yours?"

"Oh yes," the boy replied. "My mother packed food for me. She did not want me to get hungry."

Andrew grinned. "Mothers are smart like that."

The boy laughed. "My mother made flatbread from barley flour just this morning. I have five loaves. I also have two dried fish," he said, unwrapping the cloth that held his meal. "Would you like some?"

Andrew nodded. "The Master is looking for food. Would you be willing to share with him?"

The boy quickly handed the basket to Andrew. "This is for Yeshua, the Great Teacher? Oh, let him have all of it. I can eat when I get home."

"Thank you," Andrew said, taking the basket, "the Master will be grateful." Andrew walked back to where Philip and Yeshua were. "Master, a young lad offered to give this to you. It has five small rounds of flatbread made of barley flour and two dried fish."

Grinning, Yeshua took the basket. "Let the boy know I will share it with him." He then paused and said to the others. "Tell the people to sit in groups of about fifty."

When the people were organized, Yeshua held up his hands and looked toward heaven. Taking one of the barley loaves in his hands, he prayed, "We praise you, Lord, our God, who is King of all the universe. You have created all the food of the earth." As Yeshua broke the bread into pieces, El-Shaddai encircled around him. Yahweh's power combined with Yeshua's. As Yeshua continued to break the bread and hand it to his followers, the basket stayed full. The fish also multiplied in his hands. He who had supplied the children of Israel with manna now supplied his people with food in their time of need.

As the people ate, they talked about the stories Yeshua had told throughout the day. They also shared their amazement at the miracle they were experiencing. Andrew approached Yeshua. "Master, what should we do with the leftover food?"

Yeshua smiled, "Have the people take it home and share it with their friends and family. When they do so, they will have the opportunity to share the good news of God's kingdom." He paused, "Then take whatever the people do not need and collect it in baskets and share it with the poor."

By now it was toward evening, and the people needed to return to their homes. The twelve baskets of leftover food were taken by willing people who agreed to share it with the poor in their town. As the people were leaving, the young lad approached Yeshua. Yeshua handed the boy his basket, which was still full of enough food for him and his mother for the next day.

"Thank you for sharing your meal with us today," Yeshua said graciously.

"Sir," the boy replied, "I did not do much. I just gave you the little I had. You did the rest."

Yeshua placed his hand on the young boy's shoulder. "You are young and seem little in your eyes. But in God's hands, you can do great things for him."

The young lad started to go, but then he looked back at Yeshua. "I can hardly wait to share this with my mother. I know she will be proud when I tell her I shared my food with you, but wait till she hears that you shared it with everyone else. She has never cooked for a crowd like this before." Grinning, he turned and ran down the path toward his home.

*****

Yeshua sat on a rock in a small village in the region of Batanea. His followers were gathered around him as usual. A crowd of villagers sat or stood listening to Yeshua's stories. Many people had heard of Yeshua's miracles and had come for healing.

As Yeshua was preaching, a man came running up to where the crowd was gathered. He was a courier, carrying both written or verbal messages. The crowd parted so he could get through. Coming to Yeshua, he spoke softly. "I have a message from Mary and Martha of Bethany. Your dearest friend Lazarus is very sick."

Yeshua excused himself and walked a little ways from the crowd. He motioned for the courier to wait for his answer. He knew the message had come through several couriers, for Batanea was about a four-day journey from Bethany.

Yeshua looked upward. *Father, is Lazarus still alive?*

Yahweh moved close to his son. *Yes, but he is very sick. He will die in two days.*

Yeshua's shoulder's sagged. Lazarus was one of his closest friends. But Yahweh wasn't done speaking. *Yeshua, Lazarus' work on earth is not done, but he must die in order to bring honor and glory to my name. You must go and raise him from the dead. Then his life will be a living testament to the power of God. He will win many more people to the kingdom of God because of his death.*

Some may still doubt the miracle, Yeshua thoughtfully prayed. *Jairus' daughter was only dead a short time. Rumors spread that she wasn't really dead.*

You know that Jewish thought holds that three days after a person has expired, they are truly dead, Yahweh commented.

That is true, Yeshua agreed. *So it is your wish for me to be there after Lazarus has been buried at least three days?*

Yes, Yahweh said.

I wish I could be there with his sisters. Yeshua knew the pain Mary and Martha would experience when their brother died. *Please be close to them, El-Shaddai.*

I will, El-Shaddai responded. *Several guardian angels have already been sent as well.*

Thank you, Yeshua said. *I will be with them through prayer.*

Knowing his answer, Yeshua approached the courier. *Tell them that Lazarus' sickness will not ultimately lead to death. It will be an occasion to show God's glory through the Son of man.*

Two days later El-Shaddai approached Yeshua, *You may go to them now. They are waiting.*

The journey took four days, but Yeshua and his followers finally reached the town of Bethany. A messenger spotted them when they entered the town, and he ran to Martha with the news. Not even bothering to tell Mary, Martha ran to meet them. "Oh Master," she cried as she threw her arms around Yeshua. "If only you had been here sooner, Lazarus would not have died."

Yeshua held her close. "Martha, do not give up hope. Your brother will rise again."

Martha looked into Yeshua's face. Tears streamed from her eyes. "I know he will live again in that great resurrection in the last day."

Yeshua gently wiped a tear from Martha's cheek. "Martha, I am the resurrection and the life. Everyone who believes in me, even though they die, will live again. Martha, I know you believe."

Martha nodded. "Yes, I have always believed. You are the Messiah, the Son of God. You have come to save us."

Clinging to the future hope, even though the present hope seemed impossible, Martha left to get Mary, who was sitting in the house mourning. Coming close to Mary, Martha whispered in Mary's ear. "The Master is here." Mary immediately got up, and the two sisters ran to where Yeshua was waiting.

"Oh Master," Mary cried, throwing herself at Yeshua's feet. "You are too late! Lazarus is dead. If only you had come sooner!"

Yeshua looked around. By now the funeral procession had joined them. Flute players were playing funeral songs. Women paid to wail were crying loudly. Men were singing laments.

Seeing the extreme human suffering that was a direct result of sin and death, Yeshua was deeply troubled. Anger, empathy, and grief welled up inside him. Taking Mary's hand, he helped her to her feet. "Where is he buried?" he asked.

The funeral procession made their way to the cave that had been prepared as the family tomb. Yeshua was deep in thought. He saw the world before sin; it had been beautiful, joyful, and alive. Now he saw the degradation of sin bringing pain, sadness, and death. This is why he had come—to make everything new and beautiful again and to destroy sin, suffering, and death, the last enemy of all.

Overwhelmed, Yeshua burst into tears. Seeing Yeshua crying, some people said, "There must have been a reason for the delay. Look how much he loved Lazarus. They were such good friends. He must have traveled a long way to get here when he did." However, there were others who retorted with mistrust. "He healed others. Why did he let Lazarus die?"

Yeshua ignored the comments, knowing that the speakers did not fully understand. The reasons for pain and suffering can only be explained when seen through divine eyes. Given time, some answers are revealed on earth. Many others will only be explained in the realm of eternity.

When they reached the tomb, Yeshua asked for the entrance stone to be rolled away. Martha grabbed Yeshua's arm, "Oh Master, Lazarus has already been buried for four days. He is truly dead, and the body will already be …" She burst into tears.

Yeshua looked intensely into Martha's eyes. "Martha, have faith. I have already told you that this will be for the glory of God. You will see God's power through me."

A few strong men reluctantly followed his request and moved the stone away from the entrance of the cave.

Yahweh and El-Shaddai moved close to Yeshua as he looked up to heaven. His voice was clear and strong. "Thank you, Father, that you have already heard me and answered my prayer. I have been waiting for the time when you will fulfill it."

Yeshua's hands had calmed the storm, cast out demons, and healed the sick. Now Yeshua raised his hands toward the tomb where Lazarus's body lay. Power emanated from his body as Yahweh and El-Shaddai's power joined with his. Divinity shone from him, and authority rang in his voice as it echoed through the hills. "Lazarus, come out!"

A deafening silence hung over the crowd. Then, from out of the tomb, a form appeared. His body was wrapped in burial linen. Yeshua grinned. "Unwrap him and let him go."

As the excited sisters ran toward Lazarus, Yeshua stepped away from the crowd. Yahweh drew near as Yeshua watched the people gather around Lazarus and talk joyfully about what had just happened.

Yeshua noted, *It is hard to believe this is the same group that was standing before the tomb crying only a short time ago.*

Yahweh spoke to Yeshua's heart. *Just imagine what it will be like when you are resurrected.*

El-Shaddai nodded. *It was anticipation of your resurrection that made today's event possible.*

Yeshua looked wistfully off into the future, *I am looking forward to the end time when death will be destroyed forever.* Then he walked toward the crowd where Lazarus was waiting to thank the Life-giver.

Chapter 8

Mission to the Unwanted

Yeshua and his followers walked along the dusty road on their way toward Jerusalem. As they reached the border between Samaria and Galilee, they came to a small village. On the outskirts of the village was a group of men. They looked like beggars. Their clothes were torn and dirty. The lower part of their faces was covered. Some had white patches on their skin. Others were disfigured.

Yeshua walked toward the gate of the village and was immediately recognized. "It is Yeshua! The Great Healer is here!" As the news spread inside the city, the people began to gather at the city gate. Few noticed the commotion of the group of lepers outside the city, but Yeshua did.

"It is worth a try," one man said. "I heard he has healed a leper before."

"We have nothing to lose," another man put in. "If he does not heal us, we are not any worse off than we are now."

A third man sighed. "I miss my family. I have not seen them in several years. I wonder if my son will even remember me."

There were ten men in the group, but one man sat off by himself. Hesitantly he said to the others, "Do you think he would heal me too? I am a Samaritan. I am not one of your people."

One man waved his hand, beckoning the tenth leper to come with them. "You are one of us; come." Gratefully, the man joined the others.

Watching, Yeshua shook his head. *It amazes me how the commonality of being an outcast can destroy barriers of prejudice,* he mused.

El-Shaddai agreed. *In normal circumstances those Jewish lepers would not have been hospitable to the Samaritan.*

Adversity changes people, Yahweh observed.

"Unclean! Unclean!" the ten lepers shouted as they approached the place where Yeshua stood. Keeping the required distance from the crowd, the men stopped and pleaded their case. "Yeshua! Master! Please show us mercy! We wish to be healed."

Yeshua smiled, looking into each leprous face as he spoke. "Your wish is granted. Go show yourselves to the priests."

With faith in Yeshua's words, the ten men hurried down the path to the priests. They had only gone a little way when one of them stopped and asked, "What does my nose look like?"

"Like a nose," the Samaritan said. "Why?"

"Because your ears are the same on both sides," the man answered.

The Samaritan grabbed his ears. "Really? I have ears?"

Excitement exploded as the men shared with one another their spotless skin and fully formed, healthy bodies.

"What are we waiting for!" one man shouted. "We must keep going! I want to see my son again!"

Shouting with joy, the men ran down the road in search of the priests. Unbeknownst to his friends, the Samaritan stopped. Suddenly he realized that Yeshua was more that just the Great Healer, he represented God himself. Somehow, this Jewish God had been willing to heal him, a Samaritan! Running back to where Yeshua stood, the Samaritan pushed his way through the crowd. He was used to shouting, "Unclean." But now he was shouting, "Praise God!" Throwing himself at Yeshua's feet, he cried. "Master, I am unworthy. I am a Samaritan."

"Where are your friends?" Yeshua asked. "I healed ten of you. Where are the others?"

"Sir," the Samaritan continued, "they are your people. They knew you would heal them, but I . . ." the man paused. "You did not have to heal me, but you chose too. Thank you."

Helping the Samaritan to his feet, Yeshua looked into the man's eyes. "You risked believing. Your faith has healed you. Now you know that God's love is for everyone. Go with God's blessing and peace."

Yeshua watched as the man left to catch up with his friends, El-Shaddai moved close to Yeshua. *One who feels most unworthy is the most thankful for what he receives.* Yeshua nodded.

* * * * *

A crowd had gathered in the village where Yeshua and his followers were staying. Some sat on the ground, others brought blankets to sit on. Some stood, resting near a small tree.

"Once there was a judge," Yeshua began, "who did not serve God. He did not even care for his people. In that city there was a widow. A creditor was unjustly demanding her land. The poor widow took her case to the judge. He felt her case was not important to deal with, so he refused to handle it."

The crowd shook their heads, feeling sorry for the widow. Yeshua continued. "However, the widow refused to give up. Instead, she went to the judge every day, demanding that he deal with her injustice. Finally, the judge said to himself, 'This woman is irritating. She is wearing me out every day. I will help her just to get her off my back!' So the judge heard the case and ruled in favor of the widow."

The people smiled, happy that the widow had won. "If an ungodly judge can help solve this widow's injustice, how much more will God, who cares for his people, hear you when you pray. Do not stop praying to God, for he always answers. His timing is perfect."

A small group of mothers with their children stood nearby listening to the story. As the story ended, they moved closer. One of the women, carrying a small toddler, walked up to a man standing close to Yeshua. Placing her toddler on the ground, she spoke, "Sir, we would like Yeshua to bless our children."

Annoyed, the man turned to face the small group. Because women and children were of little value, he ordered them to leave. "Go away. Do not bother us. The Master is busy with more important things."

Dejected the young mother grabbed her toddler's hand and turned away. As she did so, her eyes met Yeshua's. This woman would not have to be persistent, for this Judge cared for his people. Yeshua held out his hands to the young toddler. Letting go of his mother, the toddler took a few steps toward Yeshua before he fell. Crawling the rest of the way, the toddler grasped Yeshua's robe and pulled himself up until he was standing, looking into Yeshua's face. Yeshua placed the toddler on his lap. "You are a determined one," he laughed. Then looking into the mother's beaming face, he said, "Your son will bring much honor to your home."

Turning to the others in the small group, Yeshua called out, "Do not stop these children. Let them come to me. You might think they are worth nothing here in our society, but in God's kingdom, they are highly valued. If you want to be great in God's kingdom, you must be as trusting as these little children are." Handing the young toddler back to his mother, Yeshua reached out to take another child in his arms.

As Yeshua blessed the children, Yahweh and El-Shaddai gathered close to them. When the last child had been blessed, the mothers thanked Yeshua. The children waved goodbye, and Yeshua began his next story. "Let me tell you about two men who went to the temple to pray. One man was humble like these children, the other man …"

* * * * *

Yeshua and His followers had been traveling all morning. A crowd joined them. Many people were making the journey to Jerusalem to celebrate the Passover. Now they were nearing the town of Jericho. Jericho was an oasis between Samaria and Jerusalem, encouraging people to pass through. On the outskirts of the village, a blind man named Bartimaeus sat beside the road begging. His cloak lay across his lap, and as the people passed by, some placed their coins on the cloak. He listened as people from the village talked about the day's events.

Soon the sounds of a large group of people gathering caught Bartimaeus' attention. "Hey!" he called to a person near him. "What is the commotion about?"

"Quiet," an old man yelled. "I am trying to hear."

"So am I," the blind man persisted. "Why are there so many people? What is happening?"

The old man spoke impatiently. "It is Yeshua, the Nazarene. He is coming this way."

"Right here? Right now?" the blind man queried.

"Yes, he is in the crowd," the old man said.

Hearing the old man's steps move away from where Bartimaeus sat, he called out, "Wait!" But the old man was gone. The blind man was desperate. He had heard of this man called Yeshua. He was a great teacher. He had also heard stories about him healing people, even giving sight to those who were blind. This was his only hope, and it was quickly slipping away.

"Yeshua, the Anointed Son of David," he shouted. "Have mercy on me!"

"Quit shouting," an older boy called out. "You are bothering everyone."

"Keep quiet!" another person quipped.

Desperate, the blind man shouted louder. "Yeshua, the Anointed Son of David. Have mercy on me!"

"What is all the shouting about?" a man protested.

"Oh, it's just Bartimaeus," another person responded. "He is yelling for Yeshua."

"The Master is very busy," the first man began. "He does not have time for someone like …"

By now Yeshua had stopped. Above the noise of the crowd and the yelling of the people, he heard the cry for mercy. "Tell the man to come to me."

One of the men tapped the blind man on the shoulder. "Cheer up! Yeshua is calling for you to come to him!"

As the blind man jumped up, he tossed his cloak to the side, coins scattering everywhere. He listened carefully. The crowd was quiet in anticipation. He walked toward Yeshua's quiet, but steady voice. He felt a strong hand gently grasp his outstretched one. "I am right here. What do you want me to do for you?"

Earnestly, the blind man spoke. "Rabbi, I want to see."

Yeshua spoke. "Now your eyes will see what has already be seen through your faith."

Suddenly the darkness became light, and the light morphed into images. The blind man's eyes focused on Yeshua's grinning face. "You must be Yeshua," he said.

Yeshua laughed. "I am. Would you like to join us?"

"Oh yes, sir," Bartimaeus said. "I have lived in Jericho all my life. Now I get to see it for the first time." Joyfully he followed the crowd as they traveled down the road.

"You know, I never get tired of seeing Yeshua's healing power in action," Gabriel observed. "It is hard to imagine never seeing anything, and then, seeing everything."

"Or living a life of begging, ostracized from society, and then being given a new life with a purpose," Yahweh added.

"I felt sorry for him," Gabriel continued. "It seemed nobody cared about him."

"Yeshua did," El-Shaddai ventured. "Our love was shown through him. No voice that cries for help goes unanswered."

* * * * *

Zacchaeus sat in his booth in the quiet shade of the sycamore tree. He watched the people as they milled about the marketplace, purchasing things they needed for the day. As they shopped, people talked, sharing the latest news or gossip. Listening helped pass the time and kept him current on the latest happenings in Jericho and the surrounding area.

He straightened his robe. The thick, intricate weave of assorted colors showed that it was of good quality. His jewelry was made of fine gold. He picked up a coin from the wooden box on his table. Gold, yes, he had lots of it, and land, and a fine house, and …

"All right, here it is." A man walked up to Zacchaeus. He untied a small bag holding various coins.

"Your name, sir?" Zacchaeus looked at the man intently.

"Jacob." I am taking my caravan through Jericho to trade in Perea." Zacchaeus listened carefully as the man described his goods and caravan size. He wrote everything down. Then he carefully calculated the price for customs of the man's goods.

When Zacchaeus told the man the tax price, the man was outraged. "I cannot give that much! I need to make a profit. Besides, I have not sold it all yet."

Zacchaeus held out this hand and waited. Disgusted, the man handed Zacchaeus the money. "You thief!" Jacob angrily shook his fist in Zacchaeus' face. Zacchaeus thought he could probably make the same accusation to the caravan owner who had probably lied about the size of his caravan or the number of goods to be traded, but the man kept ranting. "You tax collector's are all alike. Adding extra to make a profit. What is worse is that you work for the Romans!"

Zacchaeus shook his head as the man stormed off. Was it so wrong to work for the government? He was good with numbers, and early on he had helped many people with their business accounts. Yet, here he was rich and lonely. No one came to his booth to talk, unless it was about taxes. Few came to his house except for business.

His thoughts were interrupted by a group of people coming up the road. A young boy ran up ahead, shouting, "It is Yeshua from Nazareth. He is here. He just healed blind Bartimaeus. Now he is coming this way!"

People scurried to tidy their spaces. Some hoping to sell, others hoping to listen to Yeshua talk, still others …

Zacchaeus wanted to see Yeshua too. Deep down inside he wanted to change his life, to make things right, but he did not know how to accomplish that. He had heard one of his followers was a tax collector. Maybe Yeshua would say something that would give him hope.

Zacchaeus watched as the crowd gathered. He could not even see Yeshua. He looked at the sycamore tree nearby. It had a short trunk and wide branches. He climbed up into one of the branches and waited.

Though unseen to the people, Zacchaeus was seen by the one who sees all things. Zacchaeus did not shout for help. He did not beg for healing. Yet, Yeshua could hear the cry of his heart. El-Shaddai came close to Yeshua. *I have spent a lot of time working on his heart, and he has begun to change.*

The people will need to accept his change, Yeshua observed.

It will help if they know God accepts him, El-Shaddai added.

Yeshua grinned. *I think that can be arranged.* Slowing his pace, Yeshua paused underneath the sycamore tree. Looking up into the tree, he spoke, "Zacchaeus, I have been looking for you."

Zacchaeus looked down into Yeshua's face. No one ever wanted to visited him, unless it was to pay taxes, and he was pretty sure Yeshua did not owe any taxes.

Yeshua laughed at Zacchaeus' surprised expression. "Please come down quickly. I would like to be a guest at your house."

Zacchaeus climbed to the lowest branch and jumped to the ground. Brushing himself off, he now looked up into Yeshua's eyes. "My house? You are greatly respected. I have no status. You would come to my house?"

Yeshua put his hand on Zacchaeus' shoulder. "I would love to come if you would have me."

Astonished, Zacchaeus spoke, "Sir, I would be honored. I collect taxes. I have cheated people in the past, but now I want to change. I want to be honest. I have been looking at my records. I have already decided to give those whom I have cheated four times as much. Then I will take half of the rest of the money and give it to the poor."

Raising his hands Yeshua spoke so that all the people could hear. "Salvation has come to this home. Repentance has brought change. Zacchaeus is truly one of God's children. This is why I have come. To seek for those who are lost, and bring them salvation."

"Thank you, sir," Zacchaeus spoke quietly.

Yeshua put his arm around Zacchaeus, "Would you like to show me the way to your home?"

Nodding, Zacchaeus pointed to a fine, well-kept house. "It is right over there. Come, I will take you there." The amazed crowd watched as Yeshua walked with Zacchaeus down the road.

*****

It was the close of the Sabbath day. Yeshua had spent the afternoon in the olive grove near Bethany. While His followers rested, He spent the day in prayer.

There are rumors of the people wanting to crown me king, Yeshua told Yahweh as he rested against a nearby tree.

It is sad, Yahweh noted. *So many do not understand, and they will be disappointed, even shaken, when their desires do not come true.*

But I will comfort them, helping them to rise above their discouragement, El-Shaddai said with assurance.

Thank you, Yeshua spoke. He loved his disciples and all the people he had met throughout his ministry, and even those who did not know him yet. The days ahead would not be easy, and he hurt for those he cared about.

Yahweh comforted Yeshua with words of love. *I will be with you, Son.*

And I will be with those you love when you can not be with them, El-Shaddai reassured.

I enjoyed spending this last Sabbath together. Yeshua's voice broke the ambience. *Now I need to spend some last moments with my friends.*

Yeshua joined his followers, and they headed down the path to Simon's house. Yeshua knew Mary, Martha, and Lazarus would be there, and he was looking forward to spending time with them.

The courtyard was busy as people bustled here and there getting ready for the feast. Many were anxious to see Lazarus since his miraculous resurrection. Yeshua sat at the head of the table since he was the guest of honor. Lazarus reclined on one side, and Simon, the dinner host, on the other. Simon was a Pharisee whom Yeshua had healed of leprosy. Martha organized the food preparation while Mary stood off in a corner, unnoticed by the gathering.

Mary's fingers traced the long neck of the flask carved from alabaster. In it was a perfume extracted from the root and stem of the nard plant found in the mountains of northern India. Although it was expensive, the cost was well worth it. Yeshua had done so much for her and her family, and she longed to honor him.

Yeshua's voice broke her reverie. He was sharing a story about the kingdom of God. It was his favorite topic. She knew he was the Messiah. He had cast out the demons that tormented her soul. He had healed Simon who had been inflicted with leprosy. Then, he had done the most amazing thing for her family—he had raised Lazarus from the dead. Lazarus had been buried four days! Yet, he was brought back as if he had been sleeping. His miracles, his stories, his life all pointed toward the fact that Yeshua was the Messiah! Recently, she had heard the people talking in the streets and along the roads about crowning Yeshua king. He would surely set the Jews free from Roman rule. He would be just and fair. As king he should be given the honor he deserved.

Mary watched as the men ate. She wondered what she should do. Her status was certainly lower than that of Yeshua or even the other men. Not only was she a woman, but she had also made some horrible choices in her life. Because of her low status, it would be appropriate to wash the Master's feet. With devotion, thankfulness, and humility, Mary quietly slipped around to where Yeshua was reclining at the table. Breaking the sealed lid off the flask, Mary poured a small amount of the perfumed oil onto the top of Yeshua's head. Quickly she poured the rest onto his feet. As the rose-red oil gently poured down Yeshua's hair, its intense sweet smell permeated the room.

Suddenly Mary felt El-Shaddai's presence. She realized she was in the presence of God who had forgiven her and healed her. He had done so much for her. She felt so unworthy. Tears streamed from her face and dropped onto Yeshua's feet. Embarrassed, Mary unbound her hair and wiped the tears off his feet with her hair. As El-Shaddai's comforting presence surrounded her, she bowed herself even lower, kissing Yeshua's feet in worship. As the presence diminished, she realized she was in a room full of people who were staring at her. Grabbing the broken flask, she quickly got up and ran to the edge of the courtyard, hiding in the darkness of the night. She listened for the words of condemnation she had heard so many times before.

"What a waste!" Judas said. "She could have sold the perfume and used the money for the poor."

Mary's heart trembled. Would the Master rebuke her for her act? Yeshua shook his head in disbelief. He knew Judas often took from their treasury. "Leave her alone. It is a worthy act of charity to help the poor, but you will always have the poor among you. However, I will not be here much longer. She anointed me as Lord and rightly so. She has used this perfume to prepare my body for burial. This act of charity will be remembered wherever the good news is preached."

Tears flowed in gratitude as Mary listened to Yeshua's words, even though she did not completely understand their meaning. What Mary did know, deep within her heart, was that she was forgiven and loved.

Yeshua continued talking, "Once there was a man who loaned money to two friends. To one, he loaned five hundred pieces of silver. To another, he loaned fifty pieces of silver. Time passed, but neither could pay back the money. The man who loaned the money chose to forgive them both, canceling their debts. Which one of the two who were forgiven would be the most grateful?"

Simon understood. As a leper, he had been an outcast. Yet once forgiven, he had received his previous status as a Pharisee. He had quickly forgotten what it was like to be an outcast. Mary, on the other hand, had also been an outcast. She too had been forgiven. But she never forgot, and tonight she had shown her appreciation in an outward display of gratitude. Thankful that Yeshua had preserved his honor, Simon spoke, "The one with the greater debt."

Simon's eyes misted as he realized the gift of forgiveness and healing granted him. Yeshua nodded, giving him a reassuring smile. Tonight, two outcasts had received mercy.

Chapter 9

The Final Mission Begins

"It seems like it was just yesterday when Yeshua came to Jerusalem the first time to celebrate the Passover," Gabriel said as memories flooded his mind.

"Yes," Yahweh said. "It was then that he began to understand his mission. Now he will complete it."

"Then, he saw the Passover lamb. Now, he will be that Lamb," El-Shaddai added thoughtfully.

A deep sorrow permeated the atmosphere as they watched the crowd of people making their way toward Jerusalem to celebrate the Passover. The people's voices echoed in excitement as they anticipated the events of the coming week.

"No one has any idea the significance of this Passover," Gabriel observed.

"One does." Yahweh waved his hand toward Yeshua and his followers. Then, turning to El-Shaddai, he nodded. El-Shaddai and Yahweh gazed into each other's eyes for a brief moment before El-Shaddai moved to Yeshua's side. *Yeshua*, he said softly. *It is time for all things to be fulfilled.* Yeshua nodded. They were nearing the village of Bethpage near the top of the Mountain of Olives. Seeing an olive tree, Yeshua stopped. Soon the crowd around him gathered under the shade, glad for the rest, but wondering why they had stopped with only a mile left of the journey.

Stepping away from the crowd, Yeshua motioned for John and Peter to come near. "Go into the village. Near the entrance, you will find a donkey tied to a post. Her young colt will be near her. Untie them and bring them here. Do not worry if anyone asks what you are doing. Just tell them the Lord needs them. The owner will let you take them."

"Yes, Master," John and Peter said in unison. They quickly headed down the road, seemingly unnoticed by the crowd. "Yeshua," a hand rested on his shoulder. Yeshua turned toward the grinning face of Lazarus. "I was just thinking how wonderful it is to celebrate another Passover with you. Thank you for the gift of life. You have no idea what it is like to be dead and made alive again—" Lazarus continued his animated conversation, missing the strange, thoughtful look that came over Yeshua's face.

"Hey, look!" Andrew's voice caused a hush in the crowd. "John and Peter are headed

The Final Mission Begins

this way with a donkey and its colt."

"Could it really be?" James ventured.

"I hope it is," Judas spoke out.

Ignoring the comments, Yeshua approached John and Peter. Tenderly his hand stroked the donkey's nose. "Thank you for sharing your colt today," he said to the donkey. He placed his other hand on the colt's neck, running it along the colt's shoulder and across its back. "I will ride this one," he said to the disciples.

John looked intently into the Master's face. Yeshua had never accepted attention before, but now …

"The Scriptures must be fulfilled," Yeshua simply stated, placing his hand on John's shoulder. John understood. He took his outer cloak off and placed it on the colt's back. Peter did the same.

As Yeshua mounted the colt, John began to quote from the prophet Isaiah. "Let all the people of Israel know, their Messiah, their King, is coming."

"Yes," Peter continued, reciting Zechariah's prophecy. "The Messiah is humble. He comes in peace, not war, riding on the colt of a donkey."

"It amazes me," Gabriel began in exasperation, "how they are singing about peace, but they are still hoping for an earthly military king."

"True," El-Shaddai began, "but when all things are fulfilled, they will understand."

The crowd gathered around Yeshua as the colt followed its mother, which was led by John. Men began to put their outer coats on the road ahead of the colt. Excitement mounted as the crowd's expectations of the Messiah becoming king of Israel seemed to be a reality right before their eyes.

A young mother grabbed a few palm branches and gave one to each of her children. Their friends wanted some too. She picked a few more. Soon others joined. Then someone began to sing from the psalms. "Hosanna to the Son of David. Our king is coming. Blessed is the one who comes in the name of the Lord. Praise the Lord most high."

As they journeyed closer to the Jerusalem, smaller groups joined the great procession. A few Pharisees were in one of the groups. One of them, designated as a spokesman, approached Yeshua. "Teacher! They are calling you king. This will cause an uprising among the Roman authorities. You must stop them!"

Yeshua put his hand on the Pharisee's shoulder. "No one can stop what God has ordained. If his people did not announce his message, God would do whatever necessary to fulfill all things." Yeshua pointed to the stones on the side of the road. "If he had to use these stones to proclaim his message, he would." The Pharisee shook his head in unbelief as he could not imagine rocks singing. Then again, he pondered the possibility.

As the procession continued along the road up the Mountain of Olives, El-Shaddai pressed close around Yeshua and allowed him to see a vision of the future. While the people saw what was now, Yeshua foresaw what would be. As he looked into the people's faces he saw their futures. He saw priests surrounded by demonic forces condemning him to death, men shaking their fists and shouting "crucify him," and woman pulling their children away from him. His prophetic vision saw even further: the devastation of the terrible three-year siege against Jerusalem. He saw the people dying of starvation, being killed by bandits, or slaughtered by the Roman's under general Titus' rule. The city would be leveled, the temple demolished. He watched as scenes unfolded before him of those who had chosen him, even his beloved followers, were shown him. Many would be crucified, burned, fed to the lions. He saw the dark ages of earth's history and the end of time.

As the colt crested another rise, Yeshua pulled gently on its mane, bringing it to a stop. As Yeshua contemplated all that would happen in the next week and the future of Jerusalem, tears cascaded down his face. He cried for those who would embrace salvation, and for those who would reject it; for those who would endure pain and suffering, and for those who would inflict it; for all humanity, yes all creation, he wept. Yahweh and El-Shaddai wept with him, for only they, who encompassed all goodness, could truly realize the devastation of sin.

The singing subsided, and a hushed stillness fell on the people. Everyone looked intently into the Master's face. Instead of joy, power, and exhalation, the crowd saw only sorrow, intensity, and mourning. "Oh Jerusalem," Yeshua cried through his tears. "If only you could see what you need for true peace. But you want what is immediate instead of what is eternal. Even in the lifetime of many of you here today, there will be enemies who will devastate this city. The temple will be destroyed. Your children will be killed. If only you could understand the way to your salvation."

Moved by compassion, some of the women began to cry with him. A young girl tugged on her mother's sleeve. "Mama," she looked up into her mother's face, "why is Yeshua crying?"

Her mother gently wiped a tear from her eyes. "He is a prophet. He has seen a vision of bad things to come."

"Oh." The little girl stepped toward Yeshua, earnestly pulling on his sleeve. "If bad things are coming, we must pray."

Yeshua reached toward her. Cradling her face in his hands, he looked gently into her eyes. "Yes, my child. Pray with all your heart. Never stop trusting God."

The child nodded. Softly she began to sing, "I lift my eyes to you, my God who reigns in heaven. We keep looking to you."

Yeshua nudged the young colt forward, and the group continued singing from the psalms of assents. As they neared Jerusalem's gate, a Roman guard stepped forward. "Sir, there seems to be concern that your group is planning an uprising against the government. Please tell me what to answer the authorities."

Yeshua waved his hand toward the children. "Listen, they are singing songs of praise that are normally sung every Passover celebration. As for my purpose, tell the authorities they do not have to worry. I will not be ruling on an earthly throne."

"Thank you." The guard nodded and motioned for others to let the crowd enter. The procession continued until they reached the temple. Yeshua dismounted, allowing the donkey and her colt to rest under a sycamore tree. The crowd spread out as people headed toward the temple. They excitedly talked about the day's events. Hope of crowning a king on David's throne was the topic of many conversations. Many wondered who this Yeshua of Nazareth was. A prophet? The Messiah? A king?

Meanwhile, Yeshua slipped away and found a secluded spot in the temple where few people were gathered. He knew this was the very place he had come as a young boy seeking the meaning of his mission. Now, he sought strength to complete it. Slowly he sank to the ground, resting by one of the columns. Yahweh pressed close to his son, while El-Shaddai encircled them with his presence, contemplating the events that were soon to come.

Sometime later, Yeshua's followers found him. John approached Yeshua. "Master, the people are looking for you. What would you like to do?"

Wearily, Yeshua rose to his feet. "Our work is done for today. Let's go back to Bethany for the night." Taking the less-traveled streets, they left the city, returning the donkey and her colt along the way.

Meanwhile, the temple was in an uproar. Rulers were plotting to catch Yeshua. Many people had come to be healed. Still others were planning a coronation ceremony to force him to be crowned king. Everyone searched diligently for him but could not find him.

*****

The sun was just stretching its rays above the horizon as Yeshua stepped into the house where he and his followers were staying. He had spent the night in prayer. In his humanity he, as the second Adam, must rely on Yahweh and El-Shaddai's power rather than his own. As the culmination of the mission drew nearer, Yeshua knew its success depended on the unique blending of the Three.

His followers joined him as they walked along the path toward Jerusalem. As they neared the village of Bethpage, Yeshua spoke, "This is the town of early figs. I would love to taste one of those ripening figs."

Looking around, Yeshua selected a nearby fig tree.

"That tree should have some," Andrew concluded. "The leaves are already forming, and everyone knows that fig trees grow their fruit first before the leaves."

Yeshua held out a branch and showed it to his friends.

"That is strange," John mused. "This tree doesn't have any fruit."

Yeshua inspected the branch. "You are right. This tree has been fed, watered, pruned, and tenderly cared for. However, when the wind gently blew pollen necessary for making fruit, this tree closed itself and refused it. Now the leaves are a lie, trying to make us believe it has fruit."

"But without fruit, the world goes hungry," Andrew sighed.

"Yes," Yeshua continued. "Just as I must stay connected to my Father, so you must stay connected to me. Then you will bear fruit." Pointing to the fig tree, he continued, "This tree is like those who reject me. Without me, you cannot be connected to the Father." Turning to the fig tree Yeshua spoke firmly. "You will be a lesson to those who have not chosen me. You will never bear fruit again."

"Look!" Peter marveled. "Look at the tree. Its leaves are starting to shrivel up!"

"Do not be shocked, Peter. If you are connected with the Father, then your faith, even though it is as small as a mustard seed, will make it possible for you to do this and even greater things. With faith even obstacles as big as mountains will be thrown into the sea."

"Master, how can this be possible?" Peter ventured.

"If it is God's will, it will happen," Yeshua responded. "Pray and believe. Then you will be astonished by the wonderful things God will do in and through you."

Thoughtfully Yeshua and his followers went down the mountain toward Jerusalem. It was the same road they had walked the day before, only this time, more quiet and subdued. Even so, his followers discussed among themselves yesterday's events. What did they mean? Was their Master actually going to set up his kingdom soon?

* * * * *

Yeshua climbed the southern steps to the temple, walked through the double gates, then ascended up the steps and into the Royal Stoa, a long hallway with four rows. One hundred sixty-two massive columns marked the rows. Slowly Yeshua wandered down the long center corridor. On his left, near the entrance, he saw people lined up in front of a table. It was here that people came to exchange their money for the Tyrian shekel, a coin minted without symbols to the government or pagan ideals. As Yeshua watched, some of the moneychangers took advantage of the poor and uneducated by giving them a smaller amount rather than an equivalent value of their hard-earned money.

Unseen, Yahweh and El-Shaddai also watched closely.

"I do not understand humans sometimes," Gabriel observed. "How can they exploit the poor? Look at that couple over there. They worked all year to save enough money to come celebrate the Passover."

"I know," El-Shaddai sighed. "It is so sad when humans do not see the value of other humans like we do. To us, there is no status. All are loved the same."

The Final Mission Begins

Yeshua watched a young man argue with the seller over the price of the lamb he was purchasing for Passover.

"He is as bad as the money changers," Gabriel mused. "It seems he wants to cheat God out of offerings by paying less than the lamb is worth. I guess both those buying and those selling are thieves."

"Yes," Yahweh spoke softly. "But the whole sacrificial system is about to end forever. The pure, spotless Passover Lamb is among them, ready to be sacrificed, and they are oblivious."

As Yeshua watched the scenes before him, he felt El-Shaddai's presence come over him. Just as an angel of death had pronounced sentence on the people in Egypt who had rejected the blood of the lamb many centuries before, so Yeshua began to pronounce a sentence of judgment on those who would reject the true sacrifice of the Lamb.

Taking the tables of those changing money, Yeshua tipped them over. Quoting from Isaiah, he spoke in a commanding voice, "The Scriptures say that 'my temple will be a house of prayer for all nations.' The time is coming when everyone, both Jew and Gentile, will worship God. But how can they when the temple is a marketplace where people try to rob God and steal from his people? You are using the temple as a place to store your stolen wealth."

Quoting from Jeremiah, Yeshua continued. "Do not be fooled into thinking nothing will ever happen to you because the temple is still standing. You have turned this temple, which bears my name, into a den of thieves."

Then, turning to the priests who were standing near the entrance to the temple courts, Yeshua continued. "Do not think you are not guilty. Thieves do not just use their den to store their wealth. It is also a place to plan their evil deeds."

With earnestness, Yeshua concluded by completing the passage from Jeremiah. "While you were doing evil, I called to you again and again, but you did not listen."

The place was now quiet. Resolutely, Yeshua turned and walked through the gate into the next court where the Gentiles were allowed. He sat by a marble column to rest. His followers gathered nearby.

Soon a blind beggar who had been sitting at the gate by the court of Gentiles called out. "Yeshua of Nazareth, please help me. I want to see." Someone helped the man to where Yeshua sat. Gently Yeshua touched the man's eyes. "You are healed." The blind man opened his eyes and stared into Yeshua's grinning face.

Just then a young girl pulled on Yeshua's sleeve. "Sir, my little brother can't walk." Yeshua knelt beside the young boy. "Would you like to walk?" The little boy nodded. Yeshua took the boy's hands in his and gently pulled him to a standing position. "There, try to walk now," Yeshua said, smiling. Immediately, the young boy walked over to where his mother stood.

"Thank you, Yeshua," the girl said as she gave him a big hug before joining her family.

"I love this part of his ministry," Gabriel sighed. "His heart-warming smile, his gentle spirit, his immense power—the way I remember him most when he was with us in heaven. I miss having him here with us."

Yahweh put his hand on Gabriel's shoulder. "I know. I miss him too."

The sound of children singing broke the reverie. "Sing hallelujah. Praise to God most high. Thank him for the Son of David."

Two religious leaders approached Yeshua. "Teacher, we do not want to cause an uprising. The children are singing as if you were the Messiah. How can you ignore what they are saying?"

Yeshua paused as if trying to listen to the children's songs. "Yes, I hear them. I love that psalm. Do you like it? Perhaps you will remember another of David's psalm that says, 'Lord, you have taught children and infants to sing your praise … silencing all who oppose you.'"

Without another word, Yeshua picked up a young toddler and placed her in his lap. Soon Yeshua was laughing and singing with the children. Meanwhile, the two leaders left to finalize their evil scheme.

* * * * * *

Yeshua had been in the temple all morning teaching the people, telling stories to children, healing the sick, and answering questions from the religious leaders.

"I remember when Yeshua sat in this very temple asking the teachers questions about his mission," Gabriel mused. "Now they are the ones asking him questions."

"True," Yahweh nodded. "But there is an important difference. Yeshua wanted to learn; they only want to convict."

"Teacher," a middle-aged man approached Yeshua. "You teach God's word. You are not influenced by what other people think. Tell me, is it right for us to pay taxes to Caesar?

Two religious leaders seemed to be particularly interested in the man's question. One turned to his neighbor. "This should trap him. If he says we should pay taxes to Caesar, we can say he is against God and his temple. If he says we should be loyal to God, we can say he is against the government." Smugly they waited for his response.

Yeshua shook his head in disgust. Seeing right through their scheme, he said to the man, "Show me a Roman coin."

People around began to check their pouches. "I have a denarius!" Someone reached forward and placed the coin in Yeshua's hand.

"Thank you," Yeshua said with a smile. Holding the coin up to the crowd, he asked, "Whose picture is on the front?"

"Caesar's," everyone said in unison.

"Good," Yeshua affirmed the answer. "Then give to Caesar what belongs to Caesar. This coin has Caesar's image stamped on it. Remember, he has authority over only a small part of the earth. In comparison, people, the earth, and all of creation belong to God. They bear his image. So give to God what belongs to God."

Amazed that their scheme had failed, the two religious leaders slipped away, disappearing into the crowd.

* * * * *

Yeshua sat with his followers near one of the outer courts. Here large trumpet-shaped chests were located for worshipers to drop in different types of offerings. These special free-will offerings were used for building the temple.

A family came by. Their clothes were of fine fabric with bold colors and signified importance and wealth. Standing by one of the trumpet-shaped chests, they took turns dumping their coins into the chest. Looking around, they smiled when people noticed how greatly God had blessed them.

As the family left, Judas spoke. "I bet they had a whole year's wages in those bags." He smiled just imagining that much wealth.

Before long, an older couple came by. They too had fine clothes and expensive jewelry. They talked loudly as they dumped their coins into the chest.

Sure enough, many people noticed their extravagant gifts.

"They also gave at least a year's wage," Judas exclaimed. "Did you notice their clothes were dyed with that rare color called purple?"

Yeshua's followers talked among themselves as they discussed the status of the people who came to give offerings that afternoon.

Nearby an older woman stood alone. The dark fabric she wore showed that she was a widow. The frayed edges revealed the age of her clothing. Yeshua felt compassion toward the woman. It was so hard for widows to survive in this society. It seemed evident that this woman did not have anyone to help take care of her.

She walked slowly toward the trumpet-shaped chest, hoping no one would notice. She opened her hand to reveal two small lepta—about one sixty-fourth of a day's wage. Quietly she dropped the coins into the chest. As she looked up, her eyes met Yeshua's. For a moment she expected condemnation, for her gift was so small. Instead, Yeshua nodded and grinned.

Turning to his followers, Yeshua spoke. "All day I have watched people give their free-will offerings. The amounts may have been large, but they gave only a small amount of their surplus. However, this dear woman has given more than anyone else. She has given everything she owns."

Facing the woman, Yeshua blessed her. "The widow who fed Elijah gave all she had. God blessed her and took care of her. He will do the same for you. Go in peace."

"Thank you," the woman whispered, her eyes misting with tears. With a bounce in her step, she left feeling very, very rich.

* * * * *

Philip stood in the court of the Gentiles. Because he spoke several languages, he enjoyed listening in on the conversations of those visiting. He could not help but laugh as a man told a funny story about one of his goats. As he turned to leave, Philip overheard a group of men talking in Greek who seemed to be looking for someone. "Excuse me," Philip said in their native tongue. "I am Philip. Can I help you with something?"

One of the men shared their story. "We are Greeks, but we celebrate some of the Jewish festivals. We have come here to worship God. When we came to the city, we heard of a prophet named Yeshua. Do you know him?"

Philip grinned. "I happen to be one of his followers."

"Sir," the man looked deep into Philip's eyes, "we want to meet Yeshua. Could you introduce us to him?"

Philip put his hand on the man's shoulder. "If you will wait right here by this marble column, I will bring him to you."

As Philip wove his way through the crowd, he ran into Andrew. "We need to find Yeshua," Philip told him. "A group of men have traveled a long way to see him."

"I think I saw him talking with some people near the south gate." Andrew and Philip found Yeshua and brought him to the group of Greeks who were eagerly waiting.

"Men," Philip began, "here is the one you are looking for."

Yeshua greeted them warmly. "I am so glad you came to worship with us. My disciples said that you wanted to see me. What can I do for you?"

"We have heard that you are a prophet. Is this true? Are you the promised Messiah that is spoken of in Jewish prophecy?" one of the men queried.

Yeshua looked around. Seeing a man eating some parched grain, he asked for a small kernel. Showing the grain to the men, he told this parable. "When a kernel of wheat is planted, it must die alone. But because it dies, many new kernels will come from it, and it will produce a bountiful harvest. The Messiah is like this kernel, and you are the harvest."

One of the men spoke, "Sir, please explain the meaning."

Yeshua continued. "In Greek philosophy your goal is to help yourself reach the highest level of fulfillment, but that is not true. If you love your life and live to please yourself, you will die. However, if you give your life to the eternal God in service for others, you will have eternal life."

"Sir, how can we do this?" another man asked.

"You must believe in me and follow what I do," Yeshua continued. "It does not matter what nationality you are. My father will honor anyone who serves me."

Yeshua stepped back from the group, raised his hands toward heaven, and said, "Father, it is so close to the chosen time. Should I even think to ask you to rescue me from this mission? I cannot. This is why I have come—to save all people. Glorify your name through me."

As Yeshua spoke El-Shaddai's presence closed in around him, revealing the divine sanction of the mission. At Yeshua's baptism El-Shaddai's presence had appeared as a dove. During the transfiguration, it was as a cloud of light. Now, in front of the Greeks, who worshipped a variety of gods, including one that controlled the elements of storms, El-Shaddai surrounded Yeshua as a dazzling lightning bolt blazing from a thundercloud. Yahweh's voice resonated with authority as he spoke. "This is my son, the Anointed One. He has represented me on earth. My name has been glorified through him. Now I will complete my mission in and through him."

The light encircling Yeshua faded. The cloud lifted, blending in with the sky. Some thought what they had heard was thunder, others an angel, but those closest knew it was the voice of God.

"Remember this moment. God gave this to you to strengthen your faith. Soon this same power will judge Lucifer, the ruler of this world, and he will be overthrown. Like the kernel of wheat, I will die. I will be lifted up on a cross. But all who look to me will live."

The crowd around them started talking. "How can the Messiah live forever if he dies?" someone asked.

"My light will only shine a little longer. Walk while you can. Go as far as you can see. Then, even when darkness comes, you will be able to see more clearly, and you will understand."

As the people continued talking, El-Shaddai once more enclosed his presence around Yeshua as he and his followers slipped away unnoticed by the crowd. As they left the temple, one of the disciples commented about the massive stones and the tremendous artwork carved on its columns.

Yeshua nodded. "The temple is magnificent by this world's standards, but a time is coming very soon when this temple will be demolished."

Stunned and confused, Yeshua's followers talked amongst themselves as they made their way toward the Mount of Olives. John spoke up, "Remember the other day when Yeshua rode the colt? He wept over Jerusalem. Maybe he is talking about that day."

"Maybe so," James agreed. "I wonder when these things will happen?"

"When he was talking with the Greeks, he talked about judgment," Philip countered.

"That sounds like the end of the world."

"If it is the end of the world," Peter said thoughtfully, "what about his return?"

The discussion continued until they reached the top of the Mount of Olives. After Yeshua sat down, John spoke up. "When will the temple be destroyed?"

Philip did not give Yeshua time to answer before adding his question to John's. "And what sign will tell us of your return?"

"Yes," interjected Peter. "And what about the end of the world? When will that happen?"

Yeshua was glad his followers were searching for truth. They wanted to know so much, but he knew they were not ready for all the information at once, so he carefully blended the message in a way they would understand. Knowing what was to happen, Yeshua began to instruct his followers. "Let me tell you what is to come …"

Chapter 10

The Mission Unfolds

Peter and John found their way over to the old olive tree where Yeshua was resting. They suspected he would be there just as he had been these last few days. Something was different in his countenance. They felt something was wrong, but they could not detect what was bothering him. Seeing his friends, Yeshua slowly stood up and brushed himself off. He greeted them with a smile. "It is good to see you, my friends. I need you to prepare the Passover meal for us."

"Master," Peter began, "what would you like us to do?"

Yeshua spoke up, "Go to the entrance of the Fountain Gate in Jerusalem. There you will see a man carrying a water jug."

"A man?" Peter wanted to make sure he had heard right. "Usually woman get water."

Yeshua nodded. "He will be a servant from another country."

"What shall we do when we see this servant carrying water?" John asked.

"Follow him. He will lead you to the house of his master. Tell the owner of the house, 'The Teacher would like to know where he can eat the Passover with his followers.' He will take you to the upper room of his house. This large guest room will already be laid out for a Passover Seder. You may prepare our meal there."

"Thank you, Master," Peter and John said before turning and heading down the road toward the city.

Yeshua watched as his friends disappeared around the bend in the mountain road. *I love them so much*, Yeshua whispered to Yahweh. *Please be near them. These next few days will be so difficult for them.*

I know, Yahweh responded as he moved close to his son. *I love them too.*

My presence will stay very close to them, El-Shaddai said assuredly.

Yeshua sadly shook his head. *Judas went to Jerusalem for a while yesterday. I wish he would change his mind.*

I do too, but he has offered to help the priests arrest you. Yahweh's voice choked in sorrow as he spoke.

The priests and temple officials agreed to pay him, El-Shaddai said sadly.

We have tried so hard to help him see your divinity these last few years, but still, he only calls you teacher and never Master, meaning Lord.

A tear trickled down Yeshua's face. *As long as there is hope, we must never give up trying to reach his heart.*

Yahweh and El-Shaddai agreed. In the stillness of the moment, Yahweh spoke to Yeshua's heart. *Oh Son, the final events of the mission are here. Remember that I will feel your pain too, for we are one.*

Yeshua closed his eyes. The vision of his immediate future was ever before him.

You will never be alone, El-Shaddai added. *I will always be near.*

Thank you for your promise, Yeshua said, looking toward heaven. *Even when I cannot feel your presence, my faith will reach out to you and never let go.*

After a moment of silence, Yahweh sighed, *The time has come*

Yes, Yeshua said sadly. *I must go.* Slowly he turned and walked down the road to Jerusalem.

* * * * *

Yeshua stood at the entrance of the room and listened to the chatter of his disciples. All of them were reclining around a large table. Everything seemed ready for the Passover meal to begin. James looked around.

"Who is going to wash our feet?" he asked.

Peter nudged John. "Where is that foreign servant who carried the water?

John shrugged his shoulders.

"Does the owner have any other servants?" Andrew queried. "Washing feet is so menial that only foreign servants perform this task, but maybe the owner has a Jewish slave who would make an exception."

"To bend that low in status?" Nathanael questioned. "That would ruin one's honor."

Unnoticed by his followers, Yeshua took off his outer cloak. He fastened a long towel to his shoulder and wrapped it around his waist. Taking a pitcher filled with water and an empty basin, Yeshua walked to the head of the table and knelt by Judas. He gently poured the water from the pitcher over Judas' feet, letting the water run into the basin. Yeshua looked into Judas' eyes. The pleading look pricked Judas' heart. But it was only for a moment. As Yeshua proceeded to dry his feet with the end of the towel, Judas twitched uncomfortably. The act that could have saved Judas brought him to destruction. No Lord or Master would ever stoop this low—not one that he wanted to serve.

As Yeshua moved around the table, he looked into the face of each of his followers. He asked God to strengthen each one during the trials ahead.

Peter watched intently as Yeshua approached. "Lord!" Peter cried in dismay. "Are you going to wash my feet too? I am so unworthy. You are the Son of God. I cannot let you stoop so low to wash my feet."

Yeshua grinned. He loved Peter and the fact that he would say what was on his mind. "You do not understand what I am doing right now, but one day you will. Peter, if you do not let me wash your feet, you cannot be a part of me or receive your inheritance or place in my eternal kingdom."

"Oh, Lord," Peter cried, holding out his hands toward Yeshua. "I want to be a part of you and your eternal kingdom. Please, do not just wash my feet! Wash my hands, my head …"

Yeshua's smile broadened as he held up his hand to stop Peter from saying anything more. "I love your intensity, Peter, but you have already chosen me. You have walked with me for three and a half years. When one has had a bath, he only needs to have his feet washed to be clean."

Yeshua carefully washed Peter's feet. Standing up, he spoke to the group. "You are all clean … except one." Judas shifted his eyes uncomfortably, knowing somehow that Yeshua, who knew all things, understood his evil scheme.

"You call me Master and Lord. And you are correct in doing so, because that is who I am. Remember, if I, who holds the greatest honor, willingly washed your feet, you should erase all status and prejudice by washing each other's feet. I have set an example for you to follow. God values every person, and you will be blessed if you understand this and do as I have done."

Yeshua placed the basin and pitcher on a nearby table. Putting on his outer cloak, he made his way to the head of the table, the highest place of honor. "I have been looking forward to eating this Passover Seder with all of you before suffering for all humanity. I will not share this meal again with you until it is fulfilled in the kingdom of God."

Holding up the first cup of unfermented Passover wine, Yeshua pronounced a blessing. "We praise you, Lord our God, King of the universe. You have created this fruit of the vine. Take this cup in celebration of the salvation that is near."

The cup was passed from one disciple to the next. While maintaining the traditions of the service, Yeshua added new meaning to it. The disciples waited in anticipation for what Yeshua would do next.

As Yeshua picked up the herbs and dipped them in the salt water, the events of his future suffering were vivid in his mind. "We praise you, Lord our God, King of the universe. You have created all food on the earth. These herbs remind us of the tears that suffering must bring."

Yeshua unwrapped a cloth revealing three pieces of flat, unleavened bread resting on a plate near him. "This is the bread of poverty like that which fed our ancestors when they were slaves in Egypt. This bread also represents my body." As Yeshua spoke, he broke the middle loaf into two pieces, setting aside one half for later in the ceremony, and putting the smaller half back with the rest. "Like this bread, my body must be broken so as to 'feed' those who are slaves to sin and set them free."

Then Yeshua told the story of the exodus of the children of Israel with such eloquence as one who had personally been there. When the story was completed, he took the second cup of Passover wine and spoke, "We praise you, Lord our God, King of the universe. You have created this fruit of the vine. This cup represents the wine of the wrath of God." Slowly Yeshua's followers joined him as they dipped their fingers letting one drop of wine fall onto the plate for each of the ten plagues as they named them. They continued the ceremony with bitter herbs, charoset, and unleavened bread. Then they celebrated their time together with a wonderful meal. The followers talked about freedom from Roman power and the new kingdom. Yeshua, however, quietly ate. His countenance was subdued by the weight of the burden that only he could carry.

As the meal came to a close, Yeshua picked up the piece of bread that had been saved until last. "Take this bread," he said. Breaking it into pieces, he gave each of his followers a portion of the bread. "Eat this bread if you wish to enter into a new covenant with me. Every time you eat it, remember my sacrifice for you."

Taking the third cup, Yeshua recited, "We praise you, Lord our God, King of the universe. You have created this fruit of the vine. This cup celebrates a new covenant between God and his people. It has been sealed by my blood, which like that of the sacrificial lamb, will be poured out. Drink this cup if you wish to enter into this new covenant with me. Every time you drink it, remember my sacrifice for you."

As Yeshua handed the cup to his followers, he continued. "This is the cup of Elijah. His power was displayed at the beginning of my ministry, and it will appear once more before I come again. I will not drink this cup until I share it with you when all things have been fulfilled."

Yeshua looked at Judas. "I am sad because one of you has chosen not to enter into my covenant. One of you will betray me."

Immediately there was uproar among the disciples as to who would do such a thing. They started questioning each other. Finally, Peter nudged John. "Ask him who it is."

John nodded. "Master," he spoke softy, "who is it?"

Yeshua dipped a small piece of unleavened bread into the bitter sauce. "The person I give this bread to will betray me." With a heavy heart, he turned and gave the bread to Judas. As Judas took the bread, bitterness entered into him. A chill entered the room as an evil presence came upon Judas. Knowing that all had been decided, Yeshua put his hand on Judas' shoulder. "The time has come. Go quickly. Do what your heart has chosen." Immediately, Judas got up, grabbed his money pouch, and headed out the door.

* * * * *

The Mission Unfolds

Turning to his remaining followers, Yeshua continued. "When God's people left Egypt, God promised to prepare a place for them in the land of Canaan. Likewise, I must go and prepare a place for you."

"Master," Peter asked, "where are you going?"

"Peter, where I am going, you cannot come, but when the right time comes, you will follow."

"But Lord," Peter protested, "I am ready now! I would even die for you!"

Yeshua looked directly into Peter's eyes. "You know that the third watch of the Roman guards, occurring between midnight and early morning, is called the cock-crow. Though you think you are strong, by early dawn, you will deny me three times."

"No!" Peter exclaimed, stepping back in horror. Yeshua steadied him, and placing both hands on Peter's shoulders, he continued. "Peter, Lucifer wants to sift you like chaff from wheat in an attempt to reveal your faults and discourage you. You will fall, but I have prayed for you. When you have turned back to God, you will do a tremendous work to strengthen God's people."

Yeshua addressed his disciples. "You know that a son must build new rooms onto his father's house so that he may bring his bride to live there," Yeshua commented. "Similarly, I must go to my Father's house to prepare a place for you. By accepting my sacrifice, you are a part of my Father's household. There is room enough for all. When everything is in place, I will come back and take you home to live with me forever."

"Master," Thomas questioned further, "how will we know the way?"

Yeshua put his hand gently on Thomas' shoulder. "I am the way to lead you to the Father, the truth to teach you all things, and the one by which you can have eternal life. You cannot go to the Father alone. You must go through me."

Philip spoke up. "Master, please show us the Father."

Yeshua looked at Philip. "When Moses asked to see the Father, he was given a glimpse of his glory, but you have been given that glimpse through spending time with me. You have seen the Father through me because we are one."

Yeshua stood up. "Let us go to the Mount of Olives," he said.

As they left the building, they sang a psalm, "Praise the Lord. May all who serve the Lord lift their hands in prayer and praise the Lord."

As they walked, Yeshua noticed a vineyard. He walked over to a nearby vine and pointed to a cluster of grapes. "The purpose of the vine is to bear fruit. The branch cannot produce fruit by itself. It must be attached to the vine. This vine represents me. I am the true vine. You are the branches. My Father is the gardener." Yeshua reached down and broke off a dried twig. "If a branch does not bear fruit, it will be cut off and burned. You entered into a covenant with me this evening. Remain in me, and hold fast to the covenant you made with me, and you will bear much fruit and bring glory to God. Trust and never let go."

Yeshua continued. "When I go, I will send you the Holy Spirit. He will comfort you, plead for you, and guide you. He will tell you what is to come. He will empower you to do God's work. When you are expelled from synagogues, he will show you where to go. When you are brought to trial, he will give you words to say. When you are killed in my name, he will be there to give you strength." As Yeshua spoke El-Shaddai's presence radiated around him.

The disciples looked at one another. "Master, we believe you came from God."

"You think your belief is strong," Yeshua stated. "However, you will soon desert me as sheep whose shepherd is taken from them. Yet, I am not alone, for the Father is with me. Do not be discouraged. Be filled with God's peace, because I have overcome the world."

By now they had reached the top of the mountain. Raising his hands to heaven, Yeshua prayed. "Father, it is time for the mission to be completed. Please fill me with the same power and glory we shared before the world existed."

Yahweh pressed close to his son as Yeshua continued. "I have the ones you have chosen here with me. I have taught, prepared, and protected them. Now I will redeem them. Then I will join you once again. Please complete the work I have started in them. You sent me to this world to reveal your love. Now I send them out to do the same. Equip them to do your will." As Yeshua spoke, he saw people who would be brought to God through his followers. He saw the generations of those who would choose to follow God. "I pray for all those who will believe. Make them one, just as we are one. Show the world your love through them."

Yeshua, my son, Yahweh whispered softly. *The great battle is upon us. We must fight as one. Take courage, Son. Remember, my love for you is eternal.* Tears flowed down Yahweh's face as he drew near to Yeshua one last time. Slowly, painfully he moved away. *I will always love you*, he said.

El-Shaddai added his words of encouragement to that of the Father's. *Remember, you are never alone. My presence will always be with you. Always*, he said softly.

Chapter 11

The Mission Challenged

Yeshua walked with his followers to a large cave on the side of the Mount of Olives. Here olives were pressed for oil during the fall and winter seasons. However, being spring, the press was not being used. During this chilly spring night, the cave offered shelter and warmth. Nearby there was a lovely, cultivated garden called Gethsemane, where Yeshua and his followers often came.

As the group began to make themselves comfortable for the night, Yeshua motioned for Peter, James, and John. "Please come with me," he said softly. "I would really like for you to be with me tonight." The three followers nodded and joined Yeshua by the entrance of the cave. Yeshua turned to the others. "The battle will soon be here. Just as a guard stands on the wall of the city and watches for the enemy, so you must be on guard. Watch for the adversary, and pray that you will have strength to stand."

Motioning for Peter, James, and John to follow, Yeshua found a small cluster of olive trees. "Stay here," he said. "Just as I told the others, I will tell you. Please watch and pray. Pray for yourselves and …" Yeshua paused. "Please pray for me too."

Yeshua then turned and walked a few paces away from his three disciples. He wanted to be alone, alone with his Father and El-Shaddai. He needed their presence and strength. Though unseen, heavenly angels surrounded their beloved Lord. Gabriel watched intently. He could see what Yeshua's followers could not. The sins of the world were being placed upon the Lamb of God, just as they were symbolically placed on the sacrificial Passover lamb. The sins of all the world rested on Yeshua's shoulders—from the very first sin of Eve, then Adam, then Cain, and so on down throughout history. With each sin Yeshua felt a deeper heaviness on his heart. Yeshua's steps became slower as he struggled to carry the heavy burden that had been given him.

Tears streamed down Yahweh's face. Because sin is a broken relationship with God, every sin placed on Yeshua pierced Yahweh's heart. Slowly at first, then exponentially, a chasm formed between the two, for the perfect justice of God cannot tolerate the hideousness of evil. The angelic host stared in disbelief as they watched Yahweh's glory slowly ebb away from Yeshua. *My son!* Yahweh cried. *How I wish I could be there to hold you in my arms.* El-Shaddai gripped Yahweh's shoulders. As their tears blended, the light of their glory faded.

Feeling his Father's glory pulling away, Yeshua cried out, "Oh Father, Abba Father." No longer having the strength to stand, he lay prostrate upon the ground. Tears streamed down his face.

A chilling presence filled the air. Gabriel watched as Lucifer moved in close to where Yeshua was. Demonic angels were close by. Without hesitating, Gabriel drew his sword. Looking around, he noticed all the angels of the heavenly host had done the same. Lucifer scoffed. He had lost three battles in the wilderness and had spent these last few years planning for this day. He was not about to lose again. His power, his dominion, his very life depended on it. Again, there would be three attacks, only much stronger and intense. But Yahweh knew that Yeshua, who had conquered in the past, would have strength for the battle now.

Placing his head in his hands, Yeshua cried. He recalled the many times he had seen criminals being beaten. Their cries still rang in his ears. Scenes of criminals hanging on crosses outside the city were vivid in his mind. The ridicule, the excruciating pain, the attempts to breath while dying—his humanity shrank with horror.

"Abba Father," he cried out. "My humanity cringes at what will take place. I am so afraid that I might fail in this mission."

"You could save yourself," Lucifer hissed.

Yeshua ignored the comment. "Father, if there is any other way, let me know."

Seemingly distant, Yahweh answered, "I wish there was another way."

Yeshua continued, "But if not, give me the strength to carry out the mission. Help me do your will."

Yeshua's humanity sought the companionship and comfort of others in his time of suffering. Laboriously, he got up and went to the group of trees where he had left Peter, James, and John. He hoped to gain strength from their prayers, but his hopes were dashed, for he found them asleep. "You could not stay awake for one hour? You need to watch and pray." Yeshua sadly turned away. "Your desires are well-intentioned, but your humanity is weak."

Once again Yeshua fell upon the ground. His disciples had disappointed him. They would leave him tonight. He thought of Judas who had already chosen to betray him. He remembered many in history who had rejected God. He saw many in the future who would reject his sacrifice.

"Maybe it is not worth it," Lucifer interjected. "You do not have to do this. There are angels here ready to save you." He laughed.

"Abba Father!" Yeshua cried in despair. "So many will reject you." Then he paused. "But many will accept you. For, these, give me the strength to complete the mission. Help me to do your will."

Exhausted, Yeshua stood up and slowly made his way over to his disciples. Once again

The Mission Challenged

he found them asleep. Yeshua shook his head. "Just pray for yourselves that you might have strength."

By now, his strength was nearly spent. Yeshua was overcome by the weight of the sins he carried. He knew sin was so hideous that the price was death—not just death where one is raised to a new life, but also death that is eternal. Only his perfect sacrifice could save humanity from that. He came to take their place. But what if eternal death was his?

Once again Lucifer hinted, "Take the easy way out."

Yeshua looked over at his sleeping followers. His love for them filled his soul. "Abba Father!" Yeshua's cry once again penetrated the chilly night. "The cup of suffering, the cup of divine wrath, the cup of eternal separation from you—Father, if this cannot be taken from me, help me drink it. Give me the strength to do your will." Seeing only eternal death, Yeshua collapsed. Blood and sweat mingled together in droplets on his forehead. "Father," he whispered weakly, "I will always love you."

"I love you too," Yahweh whispered. He nodded to Gabriel. Immediately a flash of brilliant light surrounded Yeshua as Gabriel made himself visible. Heavenly angels surrounded him with swords lifted and ready to strike. But there was no fighting here. Lucifer and his angels had already vanished into the dark night, defeated.

Just as he had done after the battle with Lucifer in the wilderness, Gabriel cradled Yeshua in his arms. Only this time, instead of helping him drink a cup of water, Gabriel was there to strengthen him to drink the cup of suffering.

"Oh Yeshua, you have given up so much." Tears ran down Gabriel's face as he held his Creator in his arms. "Take courage. You have won a great victory. You will have strength to complete the mission. Many people will be saved because of your sacrifice. And most of all, Yahweh loves you, always."

As they sat together in the stillness of the night, El-Shaddai's peace filled Yeshua. The tremendous weight of his soul was still there, but the discouragement was gone. Gabriel helped Yeshua to his feet, hugged him tightly, and vanished.

Resolutely, Yeshua walked toward his followers who were now awakening. Yeshua reached down and helped them up. "The time has come. My betrayer is here. Let us go meet him."

* * * * *

Gabriel watched as Yeshua and his three followers walked toward where the others were sleeping and awakened them. Beside him stood an army of heavenly angels, their swords of light ready to be used at a moment's notice. Gabriel had been entrusted as his Lord's guardian, and he was determined to fulfill his duty to the very end.

Hearing footsteps, Yeshua turned to the crowd that was quickly approaching. A group of Roman soldiers carrying double-edged swords led the way. Behind them were a group of temple officials and temple guards. Some carried torches made of strips of wood fastened together and covered with resin. Others carried terracotta vessels with lamps inside. The rest of the group carried various knives and small swords. Leading the mob, Judas walked resolutely toward Yeshua.

Keeping his followers behind him, Yeshua stepped toward the mob. "Who are you looking for?" he asked.

"We want Yeshua, the one from Nazareth," the crowd shouted.

"I am he." As Yeshua spoke, his divinity as the great I AM radiated from his entire being. Yahweh stood next to his son, wrapping his divine light around Yeshua. El-Shaddai circled Yeshua, fashioning himself as a dove winged in flight, hovering above Yeshua's head. Joining the heavenly forces, Gabriel stood between the mob and his beloved Lord.

The divine presence overpowered the mob. They fell back as though they had been struck by lightening. As the light faded, the mob stood up. They had been shown that Yeshua was Lord. Even Judas was given one last opportunity to turn away from his evil deed. Yeshua would die, but it did not have to be from his hands.

Ignoring the truth before them, the people allowed demonic forces to overtake them. As they gathered around Yeshua, he again asked them. "Who are you looking for?"

"Yeshua of Nazareth," the crowd shouted.

"I already told you I am the one you are looking for," Yeshua responded. "Take me, but let my followers go."

Judas gained his composure. Determined to complete his purpose, he stepped forward. "Teacher," he said, and kissed Yeshua on the cheek.

Yeshua placed both hands on Judas' shoulders. "Friend, you have called me teacher, and not Lord. You have kissed me on the cheek as if you were an equal. You are not deceiving anyone by betraying me with this fake kiss."

As a Roman soldier held Yeshua's hands, a cry broke out from the crowd. "My ear! My right ear!" Malchus, the servant of the high priest screamed as he cupped his hands over the right side of his head. Blood seeped through his fingers. The crowd seemed to ignore the injury since it was only to a simple servant, but Yeshua noticed. Breaking the strong grip of the Roman guard, Yeshua released his hands. Picking up the ear, he placed it back on the servant's head.

"Peter, put your sword away," Yeshua said. "You do not have to protect me. In fact, a sword will be totally ineffective in this battle. Only the sword of the Spirit given through prayer will help you now. Besides, if I wanted to escape, I could call on twelve legions of angels. But that is not what the Father wants. I must take this path he has chosen for me."

Turning to the priests and temple officials, Yeshua declared, "Why are you coming to me with weapons? Am I a criminal leading a rebellion? I have been in the temple all this time, but you waited until now? Why? It is in the dark where criminals work best."

Yeshua allowed the Roman guard to bind his hands once again. As he was being led away, he looked around to see where his followers were, but they were nowhere in sight.

* * * * *

Gabriel, along with several other guardian angels, watched as Peter and John stepped up to the door of the large main courtyard shared by Annas, son of Seth, the previous high priest. The current high priest, Annas' son-in-law, Joseph Caiaphas, was also with him. Rather than following the laws of the Torah inscribed by Moses, the high priestly office was controlled by Rome who appointed and removed those in position at will. The extravagance of décor and building structure of their household dwellings showed that their family was large, wealthy, and powerful both with the Jews and the Roman government.

An older woman stood at the door. "Hello, John," she smiled. "It is good to see you again, only I wish it were under better circumstances."

John nodded. "Greetings, Abigail, may my friend Peter come in?"

"Yes," she said. "But he can only stay in the courtyard. I do not think Caiaphas' family would want him invading either of their residences."

"I know," John said. "He will be fine here."

"This way," John whispered quietly to Peter. "My family is friends with the high priest's family. They should let me in to the trial room."

"What should I do?" Peter asked.

"Just stay in the courtyard, and I will let you know what is happening," John replied.

"I am worried," Peter said softly.

"I am too," John confided to Peter. "But our Master has always had good answers. I am sure he has a plan."

"This is the plan," Gabriel said to himself, shaking his head sadly. "If only you could understand it."

El-Shaddai stepped close. "It is hard when humans miss what has been shown them."

"I know," Yahweh said softly. "Peter will fail at first, but ultimately he will overcome."

While John walked down the hallway to the trial room, Peter made his way to the fire. The cold spring night breeze made him shiver. It had been a long night.

The servant woman who guarded the door watched Peter. "Are you one of Yeshua's followers? I thought I saw you come in with John."

"Who me?" Startled, Peter turned away from the women. "It must be someone else. I do not know the man." Peter moved as far away from the woman as possible. He did not want to have to answer anymore questions. He could not believe what was happening. He needed time to sort things out.

Meanwhile, John stepped into the shadows and leaned against one of the walls in the trial room. Unseen, Yahweh and El-Shaddai also watched, while Gabriel and his fellow angels posted themselves around the room.

"Tell me about your followers," Annas' voice penetrated the night air, sending a chill down John's back. "And about your beliefs."

Staring straight into Annas' face, Yeshua replied. "Why are you convicting me of being a false prophet? You have heard everything I have taught. I only spoke out in the open and in the temple areas. I do not have any secret plot or obscure teaching." Yeshua's implication against Annas pricked his soul. Yeshua continued. "Why are you questioning me? You know that our legal system does not accept a personal testimony as valid. Instead, you need to give me a fair trial. Ask my followers. They know what I have said."

"What? Are you accusing the high priest of not following our laws?" a temple guard shouted as he slapped Yeshua.

Yeshua stayed calm, though smarting from the blow. "If I have said anything that has dishonored the high priest, please let me know." Turning to the temple guard, he added. "But tell me. Why did you slap me since you know it is against Jewish law to do so?"

Annas shifted uncomfortably. Because of his age and previous office, the people respected him; however, he wasn't the current high priest. "Take him to Caiaphas. We will condemn him there."

Abruptly, the temple guards shoved Yeshua through the door and across the courtyard to where Caiaphas had set up a room for the formal hearing. John followed, hidden among those in the crowd. He leaned against a column near the entrance and watched as the trial continued.

Caiaphas called several witnesses to testify against Yeshua; however, their stories did not match. Finally, two men stepped forward. "You know that revolutionaries have cursed Jerusalem by declaring that its walls will be torn down," the taller man began.

"It is true," the shorter man continued. "And this man said he would destroy the temple. That means he is against Israel."

"He also said he would build it again in three days," the taller man said, throwing up his hands at the impossibility.

"Yes," the shorter man interjected. "But this time, the temple will not be built by humankind."

Caiaphas stroked his beard. "That might imply that this man claims to be the Messiah. Only a Messiah could build a spiritual sanctuary."

Caiaphas turned to Yeshua. "Well, what do you have to say about these accusations?"

Yeshua knew his words had been twisted and defending himself would do no good, so he remained silent.

Anger welled up inside of Caiaphas, and he demanded an answer. "I command you in the name of the Most High God to tell me, are you the Messiah?"

"I am." As Yeshua spoke he stared deeply into Caiaphas' eyes, seeing not only the present but also the future. El-Shaddai's presence filled Yeshua, and looking upward into heaven, he continued. "One day you will see the Son of man coming in the clouds of glory. Then you will have your proof that I am the Messiah. However, the tables will be turned. This time you will be on trial, and I will sit next to Yahweh as Judge, and the judgment will be fair."

At this Caiaphas ripped his outer priestly cloak. "You have heard it!" he shouted. "This man is a blasphemer. He must be killed!"

At Caiaphas' proclamation, the temple guards stepped forward. While people spit on Yeshua and hit him, the guards placed a garment over his head so he could not see. Then someone slapped him and shouted, "Prove that you are the Messiah. Tell us who hit you." Still mocking, they removed the garment from Yeshua's head.

When he saw the cruel treatment of his Master, Gabriel's hand automatically gripped the handle of his sword. "Everything is turned around. Yeshua has not committed blasphemy. They have."

El-Shaddai placed his hand on Gabriel's shoulder. "Sin is unfair."

Gabriel released his sword. "I am sorry. It is just that it hurts so much to see—"

"It does hurt," Yahweh said softly, feeling every pain. Tears ran down Gabriel's face as he looked into Yahweh's own tear-stained face.

Meanwhile, back in the courtyard, Peter heard the commotion of the cruel treatment of the Master. When he saw a man entering the courtyard from the trial room, he approached him and asked, "What is happening?"

"He is guilty," the man told Peter. Then he paused. "Wait a minute. You have a Galilean accent. You must have been with this man."

Peter backed up. "I'm s-s-s-sorry," he stuttered. "I-I-do not know this man."

Frustrated, he turned and walked away. About an hour later Peter encountered a stocky man who looked strangely familiar.

The man grabbed Peter by the shoulders. "Hey! I know you! You cut off my brother Malchus' ear. I knew I had seen you with this man."

Peter was terrified. Trying to prove he was not one of Yeshua' followers, especially one of those in the garden, Peter cursed Yeshua, the very one he loved and trusted. Just then the cock crowed, marking the second watch of the Roman soldiers. Suddenly, Yeshua's words came hauntingly to his mind. *Before the second crow has ended, you will deny me three times.*

Looking up, Peter heard the crowd as they shoved Yeshua along the courtyard near where Peter stood. Yeshua's eyes turned to Peter. A tear ran down his cheek as he mouthed the words, "Peter, I love you."

Tears filled Peter's eyes as he raced out of the courtyard. He had to get away. He ran through the streets and up the hill. As he neared the top of the Mount of Olives, his breathing became more labored. As he walked into the Garden of Gethsemane, the memories of the past few hours paraded before him. Peter fell to the ground and clutched the sandy soil in his hands. His thoughts blended with his tears. *It was here where Yeshua prayed! If only I had prayed. Why did I fall asleep? Oh Master, I have failed you.* Lying prostrate on the ground, Peter prayed. *Father God, please forgive me. I do not understand what is happening right now. Give me strength to always be faithful to you.*

In answer, El-Shaddai wrapped his presence around Peter, filling him with inner peace. Exhausted, Peter fell asleep.

* * * * *

It was early morning when the side door of the temple opened. Judas hoped to find the priests here as he had when he met them the previous evening. He looked in the dark shadows and saw the form of the high priests. *Perhaps it is not too late*, he thought.

"Wait! Stop!" Judas cried. "You must let him go! I have sinned. I was hoping to force Yeshua to deliver us from the Romans, but he did not. Help me! I have betrayed an innocent man!"

"Why should we care?" Annas sneered. "We got what we wanted."

"But he is going to die!" Judas protested. "I do not want to be responsible for an innocent man's death."

"That is your problem," Caiaphas jeered. "We got our man. You got your money."

"Take your money," Judas cried. Throwing the money in front of the priests, Judas ran out the door. He ran through the streets, and out to a field where he fell to the ground under a tree. Taking off the rope that belted his garment, Judas pondered what he was going to do. Yeshua was going to die. His plans had failed. He was angry with Yeshua for not standing up and fighting for his own life. Judas could not forgive Yeshua; he could not forgive himself. Yeshua would give his life for him, but rather than choosing that life, Judas chose to take his own.

* * * * *

Pilate awoke at daybreak. He always got up this early, but the noise of the crowd indicated an urgent trial. He hurriedly dressed and vowed to quiet the crowd by handling this case quickly.

Pilate was a knight of equestrian rank. Although Tiberius was the ultimate ruler of Rome, he assigned many rulers under him. Pilate's mentor Sejanus had helped Pilate

The Mission Challenged

acquire his position. Even though Jerusalem was small, it was still considered an honorable and powerful position.

As Pilate stepped onto the balcony and looked to the people below, he heard the cries of the crowd demanding execution of the man brought before him. "What has he done?" Pilate asked the crowd.

The priests and members of the Sanhedrin stepped forward. "He is against paying taxes to the Roman government, and he is a revolutionary claiming to be a Messiah or king."

"Not again," Pilate sighed. He had recently put another insurrectionist in jail by the name of Barabbas. He came with anger and contempt for the Roman government. Pilate knew these rebels. They all had bands of men who stole from the rich, often those from Rome, and gave to the poor. Many times they killed people to get what they wanted. They claimed kingship and tried to take the throne at all costs. Tiberius did not tolerate such behavior.

Pilate was prepared to issue a quick verdict, but as he turned to face the prisoner who had been brought in before him, he saw a man who was calm, peaceful, and upheld himself as a king. In that moment, Pilate knew this man was innocent.

Unlike the Jewish laws, Roman laws permitted questioning the accused. "Tell me," Pilate addressed Yeshua. "Are you the king of the Jews?"

"It is as you say," Yeshua replied, knowing that he would only be king to those who believed. Yet he wanted Pilate to have that opportunity. "Why do you ask? Do you want to know for yourself? Or are you asking because of the accusations that are made?"

Taken back, Pilate responded. "Why would I be interested? I am not a Jew. Your people have condemned you. What have you done?"

Quietly, Yeshua answered, divinity flashing through him. "My people want an earthly kingdom. But my kingdom is not from here. It is a heavenly kingdom that includes all people, regardless of race or religion."

Intrigued, Pilate hesitated. Pushing aside the invitation to the kingdom, Pilate asked. "So are you a king?"

Yeshua nodded. "You are correct. I have come to share the truth about God."

Pilate paused, thinking quietly for a moment. *We Romans have many gods. The Jews have one God. Roman beliefs, Jewish beliefs, what is truth anyway?*

The cries of the crowd pulled Pilate back to the overhang of the courtyard. "This man is innocent. I cannot find any reason to accuse him."

A spokesman from the Sanhedrin called back. "His teachings cause riots everywhere he goes—all over Judea, from Galilee all the way to Jerusalem."

"Really? He is a Galilean?" Pilate grabbed the edge of the balcony and looked down over the crowd. "This man is not in my jurisdiction. You must take him to Herod who is visiting Jerusalem at the Hasmonean palace."

Yeshua listened as Pilate addressed the people. He wished Pilate had accepted his invitation. If only he would take the time to know the truth.

* * * * *

Yahweh and El-Shaddai kept close to Yeshua as he stood before Herod. This was the same Herod who had beheaded John the Baptist. He had brought in some beggars who were blind and crippled. Rubbing his hands together in delight, he turned to Yeshua. "Please, show me a miracle."

Yeshua stood quietly and did nothing.

Herod cried out. "You can save yourself. Just do a miracle."

Yeshua did nothing. He felt sorry for those who had been brought before him. He wished he could heal them. Remembering Lucifer's previous temptation twisted in Herod's demands, Yeshua refused. Furious, Herod turned to his soldiers. "Show him what we do to revolutionaries," Herod yelled. "Maybe this will help him change his mind."

The soldiers laughed. They were used to playing games with the criminals. One solider said, "This man calls himself a king, but he sure does not look like one. He is missing something"

"I know," a younger soldier chimed in. "He needs a robe. All kings wear robes." He took off his cloak and handed it to the first soldier who wrapped it around Yeshua and fastened it around his neck.

"Nice work. Very becoming," an older soldier said sarcastically.

The younger soldier stepped forward. "He needs a scepter. How about this reed?" As the young soldier held the reed in front of Yeshua, it bent in two. Everyone watching suddenly burst out laughing. The older soldier placed the bent reed into Yeshua's hand. He looked absolutely ridiculous to those surrounding him. Yet, if anyone looked into his face, they saw a regal appearance that could not be taken away.

"It is time to play our favorite game," the first soldier announced. The soldiers led Yeshua to a game board etched in the stone. It was a large square grid composed of several vertical and horizontal lines forming squares. Two diagonal lines connected the corners.

"This looks like fun," the younger soldier jeered in mock ignorance. "How do you play?"

The older soldier held up a pair of dice. "First we roll the dice. Then we move our 'king' along that many spaces. After that, we give him the 'royal treatment' he deserves."

"Sounds like fun," the younger soldier cried. "Can I roll the dice?" The older soldier handed him the dice. It was a scene they had carried out many times before. The younger soldier rolled the dice and began to shout out the numbers. As they moved Yeshua along the lines, the soldiers hit him, spit on him, and abused him.

"Father, forgive these soldiers," Yeshua whispered softly as he was led around the game board. "They are treating me the way they have treated many others. They do not know who I really am."

They can be forgiven because of your supreme sacrifice, El-Shaddai said.

Have faith, Son, Yahweh added softly as he, too, looked upon the soldiers with pity and love.

* * * * *

Pilate paced the floor. He couldn't believe they were back so soon. These Jews were really persistent. He knew he had to be cautious. Tiberius had executed Pilate's mentor, Sejanus, for his anti-Semitism and thirst for power. Pilate knew he had to be very careful or he could lose his position, even his own life.

Once again the religious leaders demanded a sentence from Pilate. Pilate stood on the balcony addressing the crowd. "Look," he began, "I still find nothing that would convict him of a crime. Herod also ruled his innocence. Therefore, I will discipline him with a sensible beating to teach him a lesson and then let him go." With that he turned and gave the orders to the Roman soldiers. They removed Yeshua's garments and tied his hands to a wooden post. They beat him using a simple leather whip that left nasty welts on his skin.

As Pilate sat on his seat of judgment, a servant delivered a message from his wife. "Do not have anything to do with this innocent man. I have had nightmares about him." Pilate shuddered at the ramifications of his wife's message.

The crowd was in an uproar. "He is guilty," someone shouted from the crowd below.

Pilate did not want to condemn an innocent man, but if he did not please the leaders, he could be charged with anti-Semitism. This man was somehow charged with the same crime as Barabbas except—.

Pilate stood up and faced the crowd. "Since this is the Passover holiday, I can release a prisoner of your choosing. Who would you like me to release? Barabbas? Or Yeshua, whom you call the Anointed One? What is your answer?" Pilate asked.

The leaders of the crowd shouted, "Barabbas! We want Barabbas!"

Thinking he might satisfy the crowd with only another flogging, Pilate asked, "What do you want me to do with Yeshua, who is called the Messiah?"

"Crucify him!" they shouted back.

Pilate was taken back. He did not expect this response from the mob. "Why? What has he done wrong that is worthy of death?"

The answer came first as a soft chant, then it grew louder as more people chimed in. "Crucify him!"

Pilate shuddered. He knew Yeshua would be treated like other revolutionaries. He would be beaten with a flagellum, a whip consisting of several leather thongs plaited with pieces of bone or metal. If he didn't die from the beating, Yeshua would be dressed in a robe with a crown of thorns and ridiculed. Then he would be crucified. *Barabbas should be the one being crucified*, he wrestled in his mind. *Yeshua is innocent.* Disgusted, Pilate walked away.

Pilate knew he had a riot forming that he would not be able to control, so he said, "Fine! Take him and do as you please." Pilate asked a servant to bring him a bowl of water. Dipping his hands ceremonially in the water, he raised them up high. "I am innocent of the blood of this man. He is yours."

Turning to his guards he commanded. "Bring Barabbas here and release him to the people." Then softly, shaking his head, he commanded, "Release Yeshua to the people to be crucified." Pilate turned and left the scene. He knew this man, Yeshua, would haunt him for the rest of his life.

Chapter 12

The Mission Completed

The sun beat down on Yeshua as the soldiers led him out onto the main road to Calvary, a rock quarry outside the city where the vertical posts of the crosses awaited their victims. A sign announcing the crime was hung around Yeshua's neck. Then the large cross beam, weighing about thirty-five pounds, was abruptly strapped to his shoulders. Slowly the long march began.

The Roman soldiers had been malicious in their beatings. Yeshua had already lost a considerable amount of blood. He was weak from hunger and was thirsty from a lack of water. The weight of the crossbeam was heavy. However, the greater burden was the one that weighed upon his soul. As he walked along the road, Yeshua looked into each person's face. Some had cried, "Crucify him." Others, like his followers, walked numbly, trying to make sense of what he was allowing to happen. Among the crowd were those who had sung "Hosanna to the Son of David" less then a week before. Women were crying.

"Mama," a young girl pulled on her mother's sleeve, "why have they hurt that man?"

Her mother wiped the tears streaming down her face. "I do not know," she sobbed. "He is good. It is we who have sinned."

Hearing her kind words Yeshua spoke softly. "Do not cry for me. Cry for you and your children." Once again, Yeshua saw Jerusalem's future, the destruction that Titus Flavius would cause, and the devastation that would come to these very people. "Cry for yourselves for what is to come. Those who are barren will be blessed because they will not have to watch their children die. Those who want to escape horrific deaths will cry for the mountains to fall on them. A green tree burns slowly, but a dry tree ignites, burning very quickly. You see what happens when I, although innocent, am killed during these seemingly peaceful times. But you cannot even imagine what will happen when this city is besieged. Many of you will be crucified. The numbers will be so great that there will not be room enough for the crosses to hold all the victims."

Yeshua's steps grew slower and more labored. He stumbled over a rock in the road. He gripped his hands into the soil, trying to get up, but he could not. Many thought he would die right there, but the soldiers were determined to complete the task given them.

A man named Simon had traveled from Cyrene, in northern Africa, for the Passover.

He was near the edge of the road when Yeshua fell. One of the soldiers grabbed him. "We do not have all day. This criminal is slowing us down." Unstrapping the crossbeam, the soldiers placed it on Simon's back and tied it onto his shoulders. Simon watched as the soldiers yanked Yeshua to his feet. Yeshua steadied himself. "Thank you," he said softly. Simon nodded. Then the two continued the march to death's hill.

Upon reaching Calvary, the group stopped by three upright beams. Two criminals from Barabbas' band had been part of the death march. All three were charged as insurrectionists. Since Yeshua was the most honored, he would be placed in the middle.

The belt, the outer cloak, and the undergarments were removed, leaving the accused in only a loincloth, since Jewish laws were strict against complete nudity. Aside from humiliation, the purpose was to expose the body to the elements of nature, including weather, insects, and even birds. The victims were commanded to lie down on the ground with the crossbeam underneath them. Then their hands or wrists were nailed to the crossbeam. The crossbeam was then lifted up and secured to the upright beam. The legs were bent and twisted into any position the soldiers desired and nailed securely through the feet.

A centurion officer watched while the two insurrectionists struggled as the soldiers nailed them to their crosses. They screamed curses on the Roman government. He was used to this, but the man in the middle, the one called the Christ, was different. Very calmly, like a sheep led to slaughter, he allowed himself to be nailed to his cross. Peace emanated from his countenance. What the centurion did not know was that Yeshua was not being forced to die. He had chosen this sacrifice. His only words had been, "Father, forgive them." *Could this man be a demigod?* he wondered.

A sign was placed above Yeshua's head. Pilate had ordered it to be written in Aramaic, the common language of the Jewish people, Latin, the official language of Rome, and Greek, the language of international importance. It read simply, "Yeshua of Nazareth, King of the Jews."

Four soldiers took Yeshua's clothing that had been thrown to the ground. Each piece, made from a single woven cloth, was still in good condition. Grabbing the dice, they cast lots to see who would get each piece.

People were crucified near the main roads as a deterrent to others who might try to go against Rome. People passing by would call out insulting remarks to the criminals. The chief instigators of Yeshua's execution also scoffed. "Look at him! He saved so many people, but now he cannot even save himself."

One of the thieves joined in. "If you are really the Messiah, then prove it! Use your power to save yourself—and us too!"

The other thief turned to the outspoken one. "What is wrong with you? Here you are dying, and you have no reverence for God? We deserve to die. We broke the law. We stole things, destroyed property, and defied Rome, but this man has not done anything wrong."

The thief looked into Yeshua's face. "I have followed a false messiah. Now I want to believe in the true One. Yeshua, remember me when your kingdom is realized."

Yeshua looked into the young thief's desperate eyes. "I promise, without a doubt, when my kingdom is complete, you will be with me forever." The thief relaxed. He could now die in peace. His sins were forgiven. Eternal life was promised. Hope filled Yeshua's heart as well. It was for this that he had come.

Hearing familiar voices, Yeshua turned his attention to those who had gathered close to him. There stood his mother, tears streaming down her face. She could not understand what was happening. "Mother," Yeshua said gently, "tell me about my birth."

"An angel came to me," she began. "And shepherds, and wise men." The memories flowed as she spoke.

"Tell me about when I was dedicated," Yeshua encouraged.

"The priest dedicated you like any other child." She paused.

"And then …" Yeshua prodded.

Mary laughed through her tears. "This man came up and blessed you."

"What did he say?" Yeshua questioned.

Mary knew. She had recited the words many times so she would not forget. "He called you the Redeemer. He said you would be accepted by many people, but rejected by many more."

"Yes," Yeshua nodded. "And when this happens …"

"I too, will feel the pain," Mary said with tears in her eyes. While she could not fully grasp the complete meaning, she knew that God's purpose somehow, in some way, was being fulfilled.

Warmth mixed with sorrow filled Yeshua's heart. He loved his mother. She had done what she could to prepare him for his mission. She had cared for him and raised him the best way she knew how. He had done what he could to make sure she was taken care of.

John stood quietly with Mary, listening to their conversation but not wanting to intrude. Yeshua was glad to see him. John had always been inquisitive, earnest, moldable—even while his faith was being severely tested, his hope rang true. "John," Yeshua began, "I want to leave my mother in your hands. Please take care of her just as I would have done."

Then to his mother, Yeshua continued. "Dearest mother, I leave you John. He will be like a son to you in my place."

John put his arms around Mary, tears streaming down his face. "Master, I am honored. She will live in my home, and I will take good care of her."

"I love you," Mary cried softly. Then slowly they stepped away. They could see that his breathing was already more labored than before. They stayed a short distance away, determined to be with him to the end of his life

* * * * *

Mary and John were not alone. Unseen, Yahweh and El-Shaddai stayed close to Yeshua. Their glory was hidden, but their presence remained even though Yeshua could not feel it. Now, as Yeshua hung on the cross struggling to breath, they were there.

Now that he had cared for those around him, Yeshua's attention turned to a different realm. The events in the garden were vivid in his mind. He had been afraid that his humanity would not be able to handle the suffering; yet now he was drinking the very cup of suffering—every last drop. He looked at the people around him. People passing by shouted insults. "If you are the Messiah, the Son of God, save yourself!" Little did they know that they were joining the demonic forces that were present near them, repeating Lucifer's temptation again and again with greater force.

As horrendous as was the cup of suffering, the cup of divine wrath was even greater. The separation from the Father weighed heavily on Yeshua. The weight of the world pressed down on him. And yet, he was not the only one suffering. The weight of each sin that rested on Yeshua ripped into Yahweh's heart. Although he longed to be close to his son, he could not be in the presence of sin. As Yahweh's glory was hidden, a darkness came over the cross and spread out across the land. People were terrified. They fell to the ground, waiting for the doom of the end of the earth. The priests and leaders thought their judgment had come. Some people tried to find their way back to the city, but it was too dark. Gabriel and the entire angelic host watched in horror. Their Creator who had given them life was now giving up his life for his creation. They could not grasp the infinite love of the Three.

Neither could they comprehend how anyone who had experienced the true glory of the Three could go so far as to murder the Son of God. Lucifer had wanted to be like the Most High, but he had stooped so low that any doubt of his claims against God's love was shattered into oblivion. Angels stood poised with swords drawn, willing to end all evil right then. But they knew this battle was not theirs to fight.

Nature mourned the cruel treatment of her Creator. The sun refused to shine in grief. Lightening flashed in anger. The birds refused to sing. Animals lay still in their homes.

Mercifully, the darkness enveloped the cross during Yeshua's final hours. The cup of divine wrath drained into the final cup of separation. As Yeshua neared death, the portals of the grave opened before him. He saw how sin had placed chaos in a perfect universe. He saw sin's devastation on earth. He felt the chasm sin creates between Yahweh and his people. He had known at the start of the mission that only a perfect life given freely could bridge the chasm. But what if giving that life meant eternal death for him? As Yeshua neared his death, he longed to feel his father's presence one more time, just to embrace him as they did in heaven and to say goodbye in case it were forever. But it was not possible.

Tears ran down Yahweh's face. He wanted desperately to give Yeshua hope and to assure him of his infinite love one more time. But he could not.

The darkness lifted. Yeshua looked up and cried in halting tones. "My God ... my God ... why ... have you ... forsaken me?" Nearing death, Yeshua did not have the physical strength to continue quoting the despairing words from one of the psalms.

People around the cross heard his cry. Some people believed that Elijah would come in his chariot and rescue those who were near death. "He is calling for Elijah," a young man said. Feeling compassion, the young man got a cheap vinegar wine that the soldiers drank, but another man grabbed his arm. "Wait," the man said, "let us see if Elijah comes."

Lucifer had challenged Yahweh, saying that he was unfair because the law could not be kept perfectly. He demanded dominion over the earth and its people, claiming that sin made them his. Now the battle was over. Lucifer had lost. The price had been paid. With one outstretched arm, Yeshua grasped humanity. With the other outstretched arm he grasped Yahweh's divinity. The justice held by Yahweh's righteousness melted in the mercy held by Yeshua's sacrifice. El-Shaddai's presence encompassed them as law and love—justice and mercy became interwoven into one entity. The chasm was filled. The mission was complete.

In a final cry of victory, Yeshua looked up and cried out, "It ... is ... finished! Father, I leave ... my spirit ... in your hands." Then, breathing his last, Yeshua died.

At that moment, an earthquake shook the earth with great force. People clung to the ground. Rocks rolled down the hills. Tombs opened. Lightening flashed. Grasping the cross, the centurion who had been overseeing the crucifixion looked up at Yeshua's limp form, which still bore a divine presence. "We have killed a righteous man. He was the Son of God."

* * * * *

It was three o'clock in the afternoon. The priest was performing all the tasks assigned him. He loved working in the temple and being close to God. He was a common priest, not a part of the leadership, or of their schemes. It was his turn to help with the evening sacrifice. He knew the importance of the lamb's sacrifice to atone for the sins of the people. Though an unexplainable darkness had settled over the city, the priest was able to see enough to continue his task. Taking the selected lamb, he confessed the sins of Israel upon its head. Grasping the knife, he raised his hand to slice the lamb's throat, but the ground began shaking. The earthquake was intense. The priest tried to steady himself, and the knife clattered to the ground. Meanwhile, the frightened lamb escaped, running through the crowd of people, bleating as it went.

Suddenly an eerie sound echoed through the chaos. The priest looked toward the sanctuary. The curtain was open to the inner sanctuary, exposing the candlestick, the altar of incense, and the table of bread still intact. Then horror struck his very soul. An unseen hand ripped the curtain from top to bottom, revealing the Most Holy Place and the golden chest of God with its two angels guarding the mercy seat and the law of God inside. Terror struck him. Bowing before God, he prayed, "Oh Lord, have mercy upon your people."

* * * * *

Sundown was approaching, bringing with it the beginning of the Sabbath. According to Jewish law, bodies could not be left hanging overnight. The Jewish leaders had made special arrangements with Pilate to hasten the death of the criminals by having their legs broken. This would prevent them from pushing up to breathe, causing them to die of asphyxiation. The soldiers were ordered to carry out this task.

When they came to the middle cross, Yeshua's body lay still. "Look!" one of the soldiers called to his cohort. "This man looks like he is already dead. I thought he was crucified at the same time as the other two!"

One soldier shook his head. "It usually takes days for them to die. In all my years working with crucifixions, I have never seen someone die in only six hours."

"We better make sure," the other soldier suggested. He thrust his spear into Yeshua's side, piercing his heart and lungs. Water mixed with blood seeped from the wound. The soldier stepped backward. "He was already dead." Yeshua had carried the weight of the sins of the whole world. The trauma of his distressed heart, combined with loss of blood and exhaustion, had caused his death.

As the soldiers left to continue their duties, a distinguished man approached them. Near him was a small group of people, mostly women. "My name is Joseph. I am from Arimathea, the birthplace of the great prophet Samuel. I have a sealed document with permission from Pilate for this man's body. His mother, who is his closest family member, is with me." He waved his hand toward a woman about fifty years old standing in the waiting group. The first soldier called to the officer in charge.

Joseph handed him the sealed document. The officer broke the seal and read the notice. "This is definitely from Pilate. Criminals who are crucified are usually not given honorable burials, but I am glad Pilate is making an exception for this man." He paused in recollection. "There was something different about him."

Joseph thanked them and proceeded to direct the burial process. He nodded toward four slaves who approached the cross carrying a large linen cloth. The soldiers took Yeshua's body down from the cross and placed it in the cloth. The slaves wrapped the ends of the cloth around two long poles. This enabled them to transport Yeshua's body without touching it. Touching a corpse would make them unclean.

Joseph was a rich man who owned a tomb near the garden close to Calvary. Crucified criminals were not allowed family plots, so Yeshua could not be buried with his earthly father's family. However, Joseph's tomb had just been excavated, carved from the rock quarry surrounding Calvary; therefore, Yeshua could be buried there.

Yahweh watched as the small company carried his son's body. El-Shaddai circulated among the people trying to bring comfort to their shattered hearts. Gabriel followed. Seeing his Creator so still and lifeless filled him with pain he had never known.

Nicodemus was waiting by the tomb as the small group arrived. Both he and Joseph were part of the Sanhedrin. However, they were Yeshua's followers and did not condone the evil schemes against him. Nicodemus, also wealthy, had purchased seventy-five pounds of myrrh that had been ground and mixed with powdered sandalwood.

The rolling stone was set back as the company entered the tomb. Near the entrance was a bench carved from stone. This was where the bodies were placed to be prepared for burial. Later, the bodies were placed in one of the niches or chambers carved into the rock walls of the tomb. There, the bodies rested until only the bones remained. Then, the bones would be placed in stone boxes called ossuaries.

Carefully the slaves placed Yeshua's body on the stone bench. The spices were placed in the linen. Then each side of the cloth was wrapped over his body. A small cloth was placed over his face. Nicodemus recited a short prayer. "It is the best we can do before sundown," he said to Mary. The group walked outside and rolled the stone over the entrance to keep animals from entering. Joseph walked close to Mary. "We will come Sunday morning and complete the burial process. It is the least we can do for the Master."

"Thank you," Mary said. "Once again I am indebted to those of significant status." She smiled through her tears. "The last time I was given myrrh, kings from the East had come …"

"You must tell us the story," Nicodemus said.

"Yes," agreed Joseph as the small group left the tomb site. As they walked, they listened to Mary share stories from Yeshua's life.

Meanwhile, Yahweh lingered in the tomb. "Rest, my son," he spoke gently. "Morning will soon come."

El-Shaddai gently squeezed Yahweh's hand. "Yes, soon."

Gabriel stood quietly with a group of heavenly angels surrounding Yeshua's body. "It is strange to watch over the one who watched over all …" A tear trickled down his face. Yahweh gently wiped away the tear as Gabriel continued. "It is so hard to see how low he stepped, how much he gave. But then, he knew the cost."

Yahweh nodded.

* * * * *

Caiaphas and Annas paced outside Pilate's residence. Entering would cause them to break the Sabbath. "He is dead. Why does he haunt me now even more than before?" Caiaphas said.

Annas wrung his hands together. "They buried him in a tomb. That is good. We know where the body is."

"Yes, but …" Caiaphas counted his steps before turning around. "He said he would build the temple in three days. What if the temple he was talking about was his body, you know, one built without hands?"

"Then we just helped him fulfill his prophecy," Annas said with a sigh. He clasped his hands together to keep them still. "Prophets have raised others from the dead. But how could anyone raise himself?"

"It is the Sabbath," Pilate called from the balcony. "I thought you two would be keeping your Sabbath by resting, maybe even rejoicing." Sarcasm echoed in his voice.

"Yes, well," Annas spoke uncomfortably. "You see, there is this problem—"

* * * * *

Soldiers stood by the stone covering the door to the tomb where Yeshua lay. Carefully they sealed the stone with clay. Then they secured the rolling stone and the entrance with cords. Then they placed hot wax over the blocked entrance and stamped it with the Roman seal.

"That should keep people out," a tall lanky soldier told his cohorts. "Any attempts to steal the body will break the seal."

"If they can get past us," a stocky soldier replied as they stood at their posts watching over the sealed tomb. "It is not like we are fighting an army."

The tall soldier laughed.

Little did they know how huge the unseen army that surrounded them was, for Lucifer and his evil angels encircled the tomb, hoping desperately to keep it sealed forever. Yet, an even greater army stood on guard with swords ready. Heavenly angels surrounded the tomb, while others guarded from within.

Chapter 13

The Mission Triumphant

Heaven was silent that day in reverence of the one who rested in the tomb. Songs of praise were transformed into thoughtful prayer. Even the planets and stars seemed to hum softer. As the Sabbath ended, the sun dropped over the horizon, painting the sky with pastel hues. The moon took its place in the darkness of night. Time moved slowly until the sun began to announce the dawn of a new day.

Seraphim and cherubim joined the heavenly angels that were already posted outside the tomb. Gabriel looked eagerly into Yahweh's eyes. Yahweh and El-Shaddai knowingly looked at each other. Turning to Gabriel, Yahweh nodded. His smile matched the twinkle in his eyes. A violent earthquake shook the ground, and Gabriel made himself visible to humanity. Light flashed from his very being. Another angel joined Gabriel beside the tomb. The soldiers guarding the tomb froze and dropped to the ground in total fear. The angel rolled away the stone. Standing before the tomb, the two angels raised their golden trumpets with one sustaining blast.

"Son of God, awake." Yahweh announced, authority ringing in his melodious voice. His presence filled the tomb as El-Shaddai's presence encircled Yeshua's body, which was still lying on the stone bench. Light emanated from Yeshua's form, blending itself with Yahweh and El-Shaddai as his mortal body transformed into an immortal one. As Yahweh's hand grasped Yeshua's and pulled him upward, the fine linen cloth fell from his glorified body and was replaced by a glorious robe of light. El-Shaddai enclosed around them as the Three embraced with tears of joy streaming down their faces. As the light faded, Yeshua stood alone with Gabriel and the other angel who were now standing near the entrance of the tomb.

Gabriel gave Yeshua an endearing hug. Then, gaining his composure, he grinned. "There are a few more angels anxious to see you."

"I imagine so," Yeshua's smile beamed from his already radiant face. "I guess I had better get ready." He carefully folded the linen cloth and laid it on the bench. Then he folded the face cloth and placed it next to the linen cloth. As Yeshua emerged from the tomb, the heavenly hosts broke into song. Never before had they sung with so much emotion. Their faces beamed as they sang a song of victory. As the song ended, the heavenly hosts faded out of sight and returned to their assigned tasks. It was going to be a busy day.

*****

It was very early in the morning when several women, including Yeshua's mother, Mary, Mary Magdalene, and Mary the mother of the younger James, made their way to the tomb where Yeshua's body had been placed. Salome, the mother of James and John, Joanna, and Suzanna were with them. They had made aromatic oils to prepare Yeshua's body for proper burial. The women came in a group, which was safer since robbers stayed in the hills outside the city.

"I wonder who will roll away the stone for us?" Salome asked.

"Maybe—" James' mother Mary began, but her answer was cut short by a tremendous earthquake. The women dropped to the ground and waited for the earthquake to stop. They were used to earthquakes since it was common for the ground to shake in the Jordan valley; however, two earthquakes so close together seemed like a bad omen.

"I think it is safe now," Yeshua's mother spoke up. She was anxious to get to the tomb.

As the group neared the tomb, Mary Magdalene exclaimed, "Look! The stone has been rolled away!"

The women hurried to the tomb. Mary Magdalene bent down, went through the low doorway, and stood up in the spacious enclosure. The other women followed. To their amazement two young men wearing white robes sat on the bench where Yeshua's body had been.

Gabriel grinned. His eyes danced as he spoke. "Do not be afraid." Then he looked compassionately into Yeshua's mother's eyes. She had grown much older since he had first announced Yeshua's birth. "You are looking for Yeshua of Nazareth, but he is not here. He has fulfilled the Scriptures by being crucified, but he is now risen from the dead on the third day, just as he promised." He wished he could give Mary a hug, but he knew it would only frighten her.

The other angel addressed the women. "Look here. This is where his body was placed. Here are his grave cloths. He is alive!"

Gabriel then gave them their mission. "You must tell his followers the good news, especially Peter." Then the two angels vanished from sight.

Leaving the aromatic oils in the tomb, the women turned back toward Jerusalem. They hurried through the garden, down the path of Calvary, and back to the house where Yeshua's followers were staying.

"Someone rolled away the stone!" Mary Magdalene cried as she burst through the door. "He is gone."

"What?" James exclaimed. "It cannot be!"

"It is true," Johanna admitted. "We saw two angels. They said Yeshua is alive. He rose from the dead."

"That is not possible," Thomas protested. "Maybe the priests did not think he should have an honorable burial and they stole his body and threw it in the pit."

The other followers agreed. Yeshua rising from the dead was too preposterous.

John stood up. "I would like to see if the women's story is true. I will go. Maybe I can make sense of it."

Peter stood up quietly, still feeling despondent. "I would like to go also," he said.

"Show us what you saw," John said to Mary Magdalene and the other women. The group hurriedly made their way along the road toward the tomb.

When they got close, Peter and John could not contain themselves, and they broke into a run. John got there first. Stooping low, he looked into the tomb and saw that it was empty. The grave clothes were neatly in their place on the empty bench where Yeshua's body had lain. John grinned. "That would be like Yeshua, having everything in order. Robbers are not that neat, and neither would the priests be if they stole his body."

John moved away from the entrance, letting Peter enter the tomb. He too, saw the folded grave clothes. He knelt on the ground by the bench and gingerly touched the cloth. *Could it be?* he thought to himself. *But even if it is possible, will Yeshua accept me after I betrayed him. I broke the honor given. Oh how I wish I could earn it back.*

Peter joined John, and the two started walking back toward the city. Belief and disbelief melted together in a chaotic turmoil in their minds. It seemed plausible, but how?

Meanwhile, Mary Magdalene bent down and looked inside the tomb. The two angels were once again seated on the bench where Yeshua's body had lain. "Why are you crying," they asked.

"Someone has taken the body of my Master, and I must find out who stole it!" she exclaimed. Too upset for an answer, she turned and ran into the garden. The rest of the women sat down by the tomb to wait. It was not safe for them to leave her here alone.

As she stumbled along the path, she saw a man standing beside a tree. Once she drew near, he asked her, "Dear woman, why are you crying?"

"Oh sir," she sobbed. "If you are the one who stole him, please let me know where you put his body so I can bring it back and give him a proper burial."

Yeshua gazed compassionately into Mary's face. She had lost hope when her brother Lazarus had died, and her hope had dwindled once again. Holding up his nail-pierced hands, he spoke softly, "Mary."

She had wanted to believe, but she was so afraid to do so. "Teacher!" she cried. "It is really you!"

"I cannot stay, for I must go see my Father in heaven," Yeshua told her. "But go and tell the others I am alive."

Mary went to grab hold of him, but he was gone. Mary quickly ran down the path. "I have seen the Lord!" she yelled. As she reached the group of women, she recounted everything that had happened and what Yeshua had said. "We must tell the others. It is true! He is alive!"

As the women hurried down the path toward the city, someone stood in front of them. "Shalom," Yeshua called out. "Why are you in such a hurry?"

"It is Yeshua!" they cried. Running to him, they threw themselves down at his feet and worshipped him.

Yeshua grinned. It was so good to see them again. He wanted to give them hope, especially his mother. She had borne so much. Then he thought of his followers. Turning to the women, he spoke, "Go tell my followers to go to Galilee. I will meet them there and explain everything." Once again, he vanished.

"He is alive," Yeshua's mother, Mary, cried, this time tears of joy. "I—I—cannot believe it. It is true. I wanted so much for it to be so."

Salome put her arms around Mary. "I did too." Then she smiled. "We came here to mourn together, but now we are leaving rejoicing."

* * * * *

Yeshua rested in the shade of a nearby tree, contemplating the day's events. After reassuring the women he was alive, he had gone to heaven. There he had talked with Yahweh and El-Shaddai about the mission. It was wonderful to have his Father's approval and know that the sacrifice was enough—the victory had been won. They discussed how he would prepare his followers to spread the message to the world. El-Shaddai would be a special part of that mission—filling them with his presence, equipping them to share the good news, empowering them to stand strong, and comforting them in the sorrows that lay ahead.

Yeshua had spent some time with Peter. He wanted to make sure Peter knew how much Yeshua loved him and that he had already forgiven him. He reminded Peter of the mission ahead of him and the promise that he would be a strong leader for God's people.

Yeshua was not the only one thinking about the events of the day; two believers who were walking toward Emmaus, a small town about three and a half miles away from Jerusalem, were deep in conversation when Yeshua joined them. They were just returning from celebrating the Passover with some of Yeshua's followers. As Yeshua approached them, El-Shaddai masked his appearance so they did not recognize him.

"Shalom, sir," Cleopas said as Yeshua drew near. "Please join us. It is getting late, and it will be safer to travel together."

"Thank you for your kindness," Yeshua smiled politely. "I accept your offer." As they

The Mission Triumphant

continued down the road, Yeshua joined in their conversation. "Would you mind including me in this intense discussion you were sharing together?"

"Sir, are you a stranger here?" Cleopas asked. "Are you the only one in Jerusalem who does not know what has happened these last few days?"

"Tell me," Yeshua spoke inquisitively. "What has happened?"

"Have you heard about Yeshua, the man from Nazareth?" Cleopas began.

"He was a prophet you know," Cleopas' wife interjected. "He taught the people. He did miracles. God was definitely with Him."

"Yes," Cleopas continued. "The people loved him, but our leaders turned him over to the Romans. He was beaten and crucified."

"We were sure he was the Messiah," Cleopas' wife said sadly. "We were certain he would deliver us from Rome." She shook her head. " Instead, he was executed by Rome."

"Is that all?" Yeshua inquired.

"Oh, no!" Cleopas exclaimed. "Some of the women went to the tomb early this morning. They saw a vision of angels who told them that Yeshua was alive. Some of our friends, his followers, ran to the tomb and found it empty."

"We are so confused," Cleopas' wife concluded.

Yeshua shook his head. They had all the evidence, yet they could not understand. "Do not let these trying circumstances determine your faith. Trust in God's Word. These things happened according to what the prophets foretold in the Scriptures. Remember in the first book of Moses when Adam and Eve were promised a Messiah? It says that he would crush the serpent's head and the serpent would bruise his heel? The serpent is Lucifer, the devil. He bruised the Messiah's heel by crucifying him. But by the very act of dying, the Messiah crushed Lucifer's head. Remember in the Scriptures when ..." Starting at the very beginning Yeshua shared with them the prophecies about Himself.

When they came to the edge of Emmaus, the couple turned to go into the village. Yeshua, however, acted as if he was continuing down the road. "Sir, it is getting dark. It is too dangerous to continue traveling tonight. Please come and stay with us," Cleopas offered.

Yeshua nodded and continued to share the Scriptures as they walked down the path to the couple's home. As she prepared the meal, Cleopas' wife listened intently as Yeshua and her husband talked. A fire of hope had ignited in her fragile heart, and she did not want it to fizzle out.

She carried a pot of lentils and some unleavened bread and placed it on the low table. Then she sat down next to her husband.

Cleopas turned to Yeshua. "Sir, your knowledge of the Scriptures places you at a higher rank than I, though I am head of the household. We would be honored for you to offer the prayer."

"I would gladly do so," Yeshua grinned. His eyes twinkled. Taking the bread, he prayed, "We praise you, Lord our God, King of the universe. You have created bread for those who dwell on the earth." Breaking the bread, as he had done at the Last Supper, he handed them each a portion. Then lifting his hands upward, he added, "May God bless you as you go out and feed a hungry world."

Immediately El-Shaddai opened their eyes. They saw the nail marks in his hands. "Yeshua!" they cried in unison. But there was no answer, for Yeshua had already disappeared.

"He was with us!" Cleopas exclaimed. "How could we have missed it?"

"My heart stirred within me as he spoke," Cleopas' wife said softly.

Cleopas stood up. "We must go. We must tell his followers. They must have their hope renewed just as he revived ours."

"Yes," Cleopas' wife agreed. "We must go out and feed a hungry world."

* * * * *

Panting, Cleopas and his wife paused at the door of the house where Yeshua's followers were staying. By now, with Pilate's consent, the priests and temple guards had started a rumor that Yeshua's followers had stolen his body. Not wanting to be captured or interrogated, the disciples, along with some other followers, kept the door barricaded.

Cleopas knocked on the door. "It is I! Cleopas!" he called.

The door opened and Nathanael greeted them. "Do come in quickly. What brings you here so soon? Did you forget something?"

Cleopas and his wife entered quickly, and the door was shut and locked behind them.

Everyone was talking excitedly. "Listen! We have great news! Simon Peter saw the Master. He is alive!"

"Simon!" Andrew motioned. "Please tell Cleopas and his wife what happened."

Cleopas looked at his wife and grinned. They sat down and listened as Peter told his story. When he finished, Cleopas spoke up. "That is so exciting. Let me tell you why we came back." Everyone gathered around as Cleopas and his wife shared their story.

Yeshua stood in the shadows listening. He was glad hope was beginning to shine through their doubts. Stepping forward, he made himself visible. "Shalom, may I join your company?"

The talking came to an abrupt halt. All eyes were fixed on Yeshua. Some of the followers were terrified.

"A ghost!" a shaky voice called out from the back of the room.

Yeshua held out his hands. "Touch me. I am real. Look at my hands and feet. I have been resurrected. I am alive as was prophesied."

The group still sat in shock.

Amused, Yeshua continued. "I am hungry. Is there anything to eat?"

There was a plate of leftover fried fish and a basket of unleavened bread. Peter reached out and handed them to Yeshua. "Here, my Lord."

"Thank you, Peter," Yeshua smiled. Quietly he ate the fish and the bread. By now everyone was more relaxed. When he had finished eating, Yeshua continued. "I know there is a lot of confusion about the events of these last few days. But all these happened just the way the Scriptures said. Let me share with you—"

Once again, Yeshua started at the beginning of the Scriptures and shared the prophecies about himself. Everyone asked questions, and he wisely answered each one. Layer by layer he prepared his followers to continue the mission.

* * * * *

"There is no way you saw him!" Thomas shook his head in disbelief. "It was an illusion, a ghost."

"No really," Peter insisted. "I gave him some of the bread and leftover fish. He ate it all."

"Yes," John interjected. "Then He told us how everything in the Scriptures was fulfilled. It is definitely true. He is alive."

"I am not convinced." Thomas scoffed. "Unless my own fingers touch those nail scars in his hands and feet, and my own hand feels the scar in his side, I will not believe that he is alive. It is too preposterous."

Peter shook his head. He knew it was not any good to try to convince Thomas.

Thomas continued to meet with the followers, celebrating the Feast of Unleavened Bread. The group was all gathered together, making plans to leave in the morning for Galilee.

"Thomas," a voice spoke gently. "It is so good to see you."

Thomas turned around. His face paled. He slowly backed away. "You … you did not … come through … the door," he stammered, staring up into Yeshua's face.

Yeshua grinned. He held out his hands toward Thomas. "Thomas, go ahead. Look at my hands. Touch the scars from the nails. They are real." Yeshua continued, "Look at my feet. The scars from the nails are there too. Touch my feet." Yeshua paused. "Oh, by the way. Do not forget to place your hand on my side and feel—" Yeshua did not have to say anymore.

Thomas grabbed Yeshua's hands and looked intently into his face. Then running his hand down Yeshua's side, he exclaimed, "My Master!" Then he knelt on the ground, bowed before Yeshua, and grasped his feet. "My God."

Yeshua placed his hands on Thomas' shoulders. "I am glad you believe, even though you needed to see in order for you to believe." Then, looking into the future, Yeshua added, "You will share this good news and many will be blessed. They will believe, even though they never had the privilege to see."

* * * * *

Yeshua sat on the sand at the edge of the lake. Nearby a large fish was grilling on the coals of the fire he had made. He watched the boat out on the Sea of Galilee. It had been there all night. His followers were in the boat, and he knew they had not caught anything.

Yeshua stood up, letting the ripples of tiny waves gently play with his toes before sliding back into the lake. He waved at the men in the boat. "Did you catch any fish?"

"No!" they shouted back. "It has been a slow night."

"Try taking your trawl net and dropping it over the other side of the boat," Yeshua suggested. "Maybe the fish will be surprised when you drag the net there."

"I cannot imagine that doing any good," Thomas said. "But we can try." He was working hard not to doubt so much.

"Here let me help you," Nathanael said.

The men turned the boat around, and slid the trawl net into the water.

"The net is moving!" Philip looked over the side of the boat.

"It is getting full!" Nathanael cried. "We have to get the net up before it breaks."

"Let me help," Andrew volunteered. Then looking overboard at the net teeming with fish, he called out. "John! James! Peter! We need your help!" Seeing so many large fish squirming in the net, John looked up into Peter's eyes. "It is the Master."

Immediately, Peter grabbed his fisherman's cloak and stuffed it into his belt and jumped into the water. Being a good swimmer, Peter quickly swam the few hundred yards to shore. Wading out of the water, Peter stood there with water running down his body, forming puddles in the sand, and looked into Yeshua's face.

Yeshua laughed. He loved Peter's impulsiveness. "It is good to see you, Peter." He placed his hand on Peter's shoulder. "There is a fire if you would like to dry off a little."

By now the others had reached the shore. Peter joined them as they pulled the boat onto the sand. Then they pulled the net onto the shore and emptied the fish out.

Yeshua joined his followers as they tossed the fish into groups, counting them as they worked. "I cannot believe it!" James looked at the net. "There were 153 large fish in that net, and it did not even break!"

Yeshua grinned. He loved taking care of his followers even in the simple necessities of life. "Let us put some more fish on the fire," Yeshua suggested. "Come join me for breakfast."

Everyone talked and laughed as the fish cooked. Yeshua had bread, which he toasted lightly on the coals. Yeshua removed the fish and bread. "Looks like breakfast is ready."

Yeshua blessed the food and served his followers. As everyone ate, Yeshua looked at each one in the group. He remembered how he had met and called each one. He recalled the good times they had shared together. He knew this would be one of the last, and he savored each moment.

When the meal was finished, Yeshua came close to Peter. "Simon Peter, do you love me?"

"Yes, Master," Peter answered. "You know I love you."

"I have chosen you to feed my lambs," Yeshua commissioned. Then again he asked, "Simon Peter, do you love me?"

"Yes, Master," Peter replied. "You know I love you."

"I have chosen you to take care of my sheep." Yeshua pressed one more time. "Simon Peter, do you love me?"

By now, Peter was hurt. "Master, you know everything. You can read my heart. You know I love you."

"I have chosen you to feed my sheep." Yeshua's face softened as he looked into Peter's eyes. "You will instruct those who are young. You will teach those who are mature. You will be a strong leader of the believers," he explained. Then he paused. Tears welled up in his eyes. "When you were young, you were able to freely share the truth, but in the future, you will stand strong for me during persecution. Then you will share in my cup of suffering, dying for me by crucifixion." Placing his hand on Peter's shoulder, he inquired, "Knowing this, Peter, are you willing to follow me?"

Peter nodded, now fully understanding Yeshua's intentions. "Yes, Master. I will follow you, even to the cross."

Yeshua placed his hand on Peter's shoulder. "Remember, I have already walked that path, and I will be there to help you through it." They continued talking as they walked along the beach. Peter turned and saw John following close behind.

"Come, join us," Yeshua motioned to John.

"What is John's future?" Peter asked.

"That is not your concern," Yeshua told Peter. Then looking at John, Yeshua answered the question in John's heart. "You too have been chosen for a special work. Your life will be sustained until the work is completed."

"Thank you, Master," John replied. "I will follow whatever you have chosen for me."

Yeshua nodded, and the three continued walking along the beach together.

* * * * *

Forty days had passed since that resurrection morning. Yeshua had appeared to many of his followers and friends. He spent time teaching them from the Scriptures about his mission and the role they would play in completing the mission. The time had finally come for him to return to heaven. A large group of followers met on the Mount of Olives. All were anxious to spend as much time as possible with their beloved Master.

Yeshua circulated among the crowd, visiting with each individual. He also spoke with Joseph of Arimathea and Nicodemus. He thanked them for their kindness at his burial and encouraged them to continue following him. He spent time with Lazarus, Mary, and Martha. He had spent many days with them, and he appreciated their hospitality. Lazarus was doing well, sharing the good news of the One who was the resurrection and the life. Mary and Martha would strengthen the believers through their hospitality. He made sure he had spent special time with each of his followers, just as he had done with Peter and John, encouraging them for their future work. He also talked with his biological brothers and sisters, for they had become followers too.

Most of all, he spent time with his mother, Mary. She had loved him, cared for him, and stayed true to him even when she did not understand. She had taught him stories from Scripture when he was younger; now he explained Scripture to her. Tenderly he explained all the events their lives had shared together. Then he wrapped his arms around her and held her close. "I love you," he said softly.

"I love you too," Mary smiled back.

"I will be leaving," Yeshua told her. "I must go back to my Father in heaven. I have work to do there, just as you have work to do here."

"I am sure you do." Mary sighed. "But this is different. You are not dying an unfair criminal's death. You are going to your Father. I will miss you, but I can be glad for you as well."

Yahweh and El-Shaddai watched as Yeshua spent time with each person. Gabriel waited patiently beside them. Now they watched as he bid farewell to his mother.

Yeshua squeezed Mary's hands and gently kissed her. "John will take good care of you."

"I know," Mary nodded. "He already has."

"Goodbye," Yeshua said softly.

Yeshua walked a short distance to the top of the mountain overlooking Jerusalem. As he lifted his hands, everyone stopped talking and listened.

"Yahweh called me to a mission. I have fulfilled that mission here on earth. Now I have called you to continue that mission. Prepare yourselves to receive the promised Holy Spirit. He will give you power to do the special tasks you were assigned. You will share the good news in Jerusalem and in Judea. You will even share it with those in Samaria. Some of you will take the message to the very ends of the earth. Yahweh has ordained the commission I now give you. Go, all of you, into the entire world. Teach them the way of truth. Baptize them in the name of the Father, the Son, and the Holy Spirit. Train them for service. Remember, you will never be alone. I will always be with you, right up to the day when I will come back for you."

As Yeshua concluded his farewell blessing, El-Shaddai surrounded him with his glory, forming a cloud of light under his feet. Yahweh joined Yeshua as he began to rise slowly into the air. A chariot of angels led the procession. Other angels circled around the Three, accompanied by the angelic choir. As they faded out of sight, Gabriel and his accompanying angel stood in their place.

Gabriel grinned. Humans always amused him. Little glimpses of Yahweh's glory made them totally awestruck. If only they could really see his glory! Then in a clear, melodious voice, he spoke, "People of Galilee, why are you still looking up in the sky? Do not be discouraged. Have faith. Remember his promise. This very same Yeshua will come again in the clouds surrounded by angels. You will rise to meet him in the clouds, and he will take you home to be with him forever."

Slowly the group turned and moved down the mountain path. They talked about their Lord, their new lives, and their mission. They were a community of believers. They would support one another and work together. His coming had changed their lives. His departure had transformed them again. Their lives would never be the same.

Chapter 14

The Mission Continues

The celebration was amazing. The angelic choir had been practicing for a little more than thirty-three years for this performance. Gabriel sung a special song he had composed while Yeshua was on earth. Creatures from other worlds and universes gathered in praise and celebration. The planets and stars joined together in a song of adoration. Yahweh, Yeshua, and El-Shaddai sung a song that touched everyone's heart. As the Three sang, everyone saw the scars Yeshua still carried from the mission. The risk had been so immense, the mission so dangerous. Triumph rang in the voices of the Three. The mission had been accomplished. They had been victorious. Love and compassion emanated from them, touching all those who listened. And now, through the mission, that love had touched the earth in a tangible way. Everyone stood in awe as the song finished.

As the service came to a close, Yahweh, Yeshua, and El-Shaddai stood as countless worshippers greeted them and welcomed Yeshua home. Once again, Gabriel waited until the end. Working so closely with Yeshua on earth had strengthened the bond between them. Grasping Yeshua's hands, he turned them over carefully, gently running his fingers over the scars of the sacrifice. Tears filled his eyes. "Yeshua, you gave …" Gabriel paused. He tried again, "The cost …"

Tenderly Yeshua reached up and wiped the tears from Gabriel's face. "Yes, but the reward was worth it," Yeshua said softly. Then he wrapped his arms around Gabriel and held him close. After a few moments, Yeshua relaxed his hands until they rested on Gabriel's shoulders. "You played an important role in the mission," Yeshua said.

"It was not easy," Gabriel responded. "I wanted so much to rescue you, but I had to remember the mission was for you to do the rescuing."

Yeshua laughed. Yahweh and El-Shaddai joined them. As they walked along the golden street, Yeshua's gaze was faraway and thoughtful. "I miss them already," he said. "I wish they could be here with us."

Yahweh smiled. "One day they will be."

El-Shaddai nodded. "There is so much we must do to prepare for that day."

Yeshua turned to Yahweh and El-Shaddai. "Shall we?" Then, utilizing their omnipresence the Three journeyed into the future, carefully planning and orchestrating the remaining time of earth. The next part of the mission had begun.

We invite you to view the complete
selection of titles we publish at:

www.TEACHServices.com

Scan with your mobile
device to go directly
to our website.

Please write or email us your praises, reactions,
or thoughts about this or any other book we publish at:

P.O. Box 954
Ringgold, GA 30736

info@TEACHServices.com

TEACH Services, Inc., titles may be purchased in bulk for
educational, business, fund-raising, or sales promotional use.
For information, please e-mail:

BulkSales@TEACHServices.com

Finally, if you are interested in seeing
your own book in print, please contact us at

publishing@TEACHServices.com

We would be happy to review your manuscript for free.

www.ingramcontent.com/pod-product-compliance
Lightning Source LLC
Chambersburg PA
CBHW082231180426
43200CB00037B/2822